Write Out of the Oven!

*Letters and Recipes
from Children's Authors*

Josephine M. Waltz

Illustrated by Christine Mix

Teacher Ideas Press
Portsmouth, NH

For Chelsea, Casey, and Jeffrey

Teacher Ideas Press
A division of Reed Elsevier Inc.
361 Hanover Street
Portsmouth, NH 03801–3912
www.teacherideaspress.com

Offices and agents throughout the world

© 2005 by Josephine Waltz

Library of Congress Cataloging-in-Publication Data

Waltz, Josephine M.
    Write out of the oven! : letters and recipes from children's authors / by Josephine M. Waltz.
      p. cm.
    Includes indexes.
    ISBN 1–59469–008–1 (alk. paper)
    1. Children's literature, American—History and criticism—Theory, etc. 2. Authors, American—20th century—Correspondence. 3. Children—Books and reading—United States. 4. Children—United States—Correspondence. 5. Children's literature—Authorship. 6. Cookery, American. I. Title.
    PS490.W35 2005
    810.9'9282'0904—dc22
                                 2004021946

Editor: Suzanne Barchers
Production Coordinator: Angela Rice
Typesetter: Westchester Book Services
Cover design: Anne Payne
Manufacturing: Steve Bernier

Printed in the United States of America on acid-free paper
09 08 07 06 05 VP 1 2 3 4 5

❧ Contents ❧

❧ Preface ❧

Although many recipes in this book were tested, adjustments in seasoning or ingredients may be required to satisfy individual tastes and needs. A glossary of cooking terms and staples is included in the back of this book for your convenience.

Also, the authors' letters are presented as they were received, with little editing. Initially, my students and I were only interested in the authors' recipes, but after receiving such wonderful letters, it became clear that they were treasures unto themselves, and I decided to include them in the book with permission from the authors.

It is our wish that students, parents, teachers, and anyone else will turn to *Write Out of the Oven!* when looking for a great book to read or when looking for an author's favorite recipe to try, be it Chinese Slaw, Penne Perfecto, or even Glop!

✌ **Introduction** ✍

It is hard to believe that in the spring of 2001 my sixth-grade reading students and I embarked on an adventure to collect recipes from our favorite authors. That year and the year that followed our reading interests were high, our curiosity strong, our determination unstoppable, and our mission honorable.

It all began with a question. "Wouldn't it be great if we could get kids new books? We are very fortunate because our school has many, many books. In fact, we can buy new books when we need them or go to our local library to find practically any great book to read, but everyone is not as lucky. We could help other kids get books by raising money for a children's literacy foundation. Our class could write a book of our own that features letters to our favorite authors and includes the authors' favorite recipes. After all, food is universal and it connects all of us; besides, it will seem like we are having dinner with our favorite authors. And if we are really lucky, we could try to publish the collection of recipes along with our letters. Profits would be sent to a children's literacy foundation that could buy new books for areas that need them and even buy books for shelters." This was the premise of our project, and while all the students agreed that it was a great idea, few believed their favorite authors would write back. But they did. And we did what we set out to do.

Students first identified their favorite authors, and much to my surprise, they represented a wonderful range of literary works. Students quickly learned the arts of letterwriting and persuasive writing. I asked them to consider why these authors were special and encouraged them to write sincere, heartfelt letters. I was amazed with the students' overall efforts and honest self-reflections. Students wrote about how much they appreciated the books and they included an evaluation of the authors' literature.

Students also researched information about the authors. They especially searched for unusual and interesting information. Once the letters were drafted, the real challenge presented itself: How were the students going to get these letters to the authors? Students used reference books and, with my help, they searched the Internet for author addresses. Students located many addresses from wonderful author Web sites. However, when they couldn't locate an address, they sent their letters to the publishing houses that published the authors' books. Students decorated their letters with spot art, signed their names, and stuffed the letters into colorful envelopes. Finally, the envelopes were addressed and mailed. We waited. After a few weeks and much to everyone's amazement, the authors' responses began to arrive.

The excitement was contagious! Each time a letter arrived, it was read out loud and we all applauded. I explained to the students that authors receive thousands of letters and are extremely busy, so receiving *anything* from them seemed to me like we were opening up a present. And sure enough the letters the students received were even more than presents, they were treasures. Not a day passed without a student asking me, "Did I get a letter? Did I get a letter?" In order to get the word out, I posted on our classroom door the names of authors whose letters had just arrived.

Two years went by and I often marveled at how grown-up and self-assured my former students were becoming. They towered over me. I told them, "As with so many things, time is always a factor; it takes perseverance, patience, and luck for dreams to be fulfilled. I know we have all these things." Throughout those two years the students often stopped me in the hall to ask, "What ever happened to our book? Are we still going to get it published?" I would grin like a Cheshire cat and say, "Well, I'm still working on it," or "I haven't forgotten about it."

Along our journey, we learned life lessons: Dream big dreams, never be discouraged by roadblocks, make a plan, take some risks, and finally, always believe in yourself. Children can be authors too, even sixth graders who are willing to write, especially for a worthy cause.

Write Out of the Oven! is a testimony to how important children's authors are for young readers. All children should have the opportunity to read great books, regardless of where they live or who they are. Whether authors realize it or not, they are our heroes. Children learn about their world, themselves, and others from authors and their literary works. Authors help us shape who we want to be. They encourage us to have faith in ourselves and to consider our future with endless possibilities.

And so we invite all who leaf through these pages to come dine with us and discover wonderful authors and reflections from young readers. We hope many copies of this cookbook will be sold so that lots and lots of new books will be purchased for kids. Net proceeds will go to CLiF, a children's literacy foundation in Waterbury Center, Vermont.

J. Waltz

✤ Acknowledgments ✤

My students and I want to thank all the authors who are featured in this book for sharing their thoughts, recipes, kindness, and words of encouragement. We so greatly appreciate their generous efforts in helping us with this project. Their letters offered wonderful words of advice. While some letters made us laugh, other letters helped us reconsider ideas. We wish each and every author continued years of successful writing.

I would like to give special thanks to the following people: my acquisitions editor, Suzanne Barchers, who saw value in this project while it was still in its early stages, because without her interest, support, and guidance it would not have gotten off the ground. Marge Bradley, for her kindness in collecting and forwarding author letters to my home throughout the summer months. Antonette D' Orazio, children's services supervisor, who allowed me to display sample letters in the town library, and all the staff and librarians there who *oooed* and *ahhhed,* even before I knew the book would be published. My dear friend Evon Martins, who helped field-test some of the recipes. My husband Charlie, who took many many trips to the grocery store to track down unfamiliar ingredients, and who encouraged me every step of the way. My children, who tasted and tried endless new recipes and enthusiastically asked, "What are we going to try out tonight?" But most importantly, to all my students who believed in our mission before we knew whether our book would go to print. Their enthusiasm directly impacted the success of this cookbook.

Finally, my thanks to Natalie Babbitt and Theodore Taylor, who have long been my inspiration.

❧ Write Out of the Oven! ❧ Safety and Cooking Tips

Safety Tips

Get permission from an adult to use the stove, oven, or any electrical appliance.

Make sure your hands are washed before preparing a recipe.

Check that all cooking utensils and surfaces are clean.

Wash all vegetables thoroughly.

Move peeler away from yourself when peeling vegetables.

Use a cutting board for slicing and chopping.

Place utensils in the sink and wipe down the counter after using utensils with chicken and meat products.

Plug appliances into outlets carefully.

Never put water into hot oil.

Don't taste foods that are uncooked.

Turn long handles of saucepans or pots on the stove to the side.

Place forks and knives face down into the dishwasher.

Set the timer to avoid overcooking or undercooking foods.

Never leave a stove unattended while food is cooking.

Wear oven mitts when placing or removing baked foods from the oven.

Turn off the stove or oven after use.

Cooking Tips

Read the recipe thoroughly and note how long it takes to prepare.

Look up unfamiliar cooking terms in the glossary.

Collect all cooking equipment and ingredients before beginning.

Follow directions carefully.

Measure all ingredients carefully.

Use a dull knife to level dry ingredients when using measuring cups and spoons.

Preheat the oven to the desired temperature.

Use a toothpick or a long piece of spaghetti to test for doneness of cakes and breads.

Run knife under hot water before using it to cut ice cream into large slices.

Cooking times may vary depending on your stove and altitude.

Spray aluminum foil with cooking spray to avoid having food stick to foil while baking.

Season foods to taste.

1 ❧ Dips

Natalie Babbitt

Dear Natalie Babbitt,

I read your book *Tuck Everlasting* and really enjoyed it. Usually I really don't like to read but this book was a huge exception. I really liked the whole idea of being immortal. It was a great combination of action, suspense, and drama. I was also wondering how did you come up with all of those descriptive words to describe the *road* . . .

Kyle Brady

Dear Natalie Babbitt,

This year in sixth grade, my reading class read one of your novels, *Tuck Everlasting.* It was without a doubt one of my favorite novels ever. It was descriptive, suspenseful, and just fun to read, even though it is not a typical book. I loved how it was so deep. It taught me to cherish what I have instead of always wanting more . . .

Patrick Coughlin

Dear Natalie Babbitt,

I have recently read one of your books, *Tuck Everlasting.* This is a very inspiring and intriguing book. My favorite part is when Winnie gives the toad water from the spring. Tuck says that the toad thinks he will live forever. This was a coincidence because the toad *will* really live forever . . .

Anyway, I am hoping you can send me a recipe. It can be a family recipe or maybe just a recipe of your favorite food. I do not have a favorite recipe, but my favorite foods are French fries, slushies, and most other kinds of junk foods . . .

Erica Habina

Dear Natalie Babbitt,

I love *Tuck Everlasting!* You took a lot of different kinds of stories: magical, action, mystery, drama, and much more. You put them together and made an awesome story. I wouldn't change anything . . .

Ashley Longosz

Dear Natalie Babbitt,

Hello! I absolutely loved *Knee·knock Rise.* I think it was the best book I've ever read! I also really enjoyed *Tuck Everlasting.* I'm actually fond of a lot of your books. I think that you are the best author. We are doing a project in class. I was wondering if you could possibly give me your favorite recipe. It would be put into a book with other author's favorite recipes. This is a good collection because it will probably encourage other kids to read more and more. It will get kids to want to read . . . and hey, maybe even some of your books . . .

Kaleigh Marvel

Dear Natalie Babbitt,

I am a major fan of your writing. I think it is interesting that you didn't know you wanted to be a writer until a little later in your life. Did your inspiration come from your husband or your childhood? I especially loved your novel *Tuck Everlasting.* My favorite part was when Winnie temporarily got the opportunity to live with the Tucks and experience the family's lifestyle.

Another one of my favorite parts was when Winnie jeopardized her safety for Mae Tuck's freedom. She helped get her out of jail and the gallows by impersonating Mae. I also thought your figurative language was wisely thought out, which made the book irresistible and nearly impossible to put down . . .

Katherine Mullins

Dear Natalie Babbitt,

I read that you are interested in fantasy and possibilities. I think that being interested in fantasy and possibilities is a good characteristic for a writer to have because then they can have many possibilities in their writings. I also read that you teach writing for children and book illustrations at Kirkland College, a women's liberal arts college. I think that makes you a fabulous role model because you have a lot of talent and you use it to help others.

The ending of your books always makes a lot of sense, especially if you pay attention to the little details and descriptions. And the more I read your books over, the more details and descriptions I catch. These details and descriptions make your books come to life. An example of a part in the story that you wrote, which connects very well in *Tuck Everlasting,* was when Jesse doesn't want Winnie to drink from the spring although he did. He mentioned he was 104 years old and if you think about it, it makes sense that he *is* 104 years old because drinking from the spring made him live forever.

I love your writing style so much that I chose to write to you . . .

Sharon Ovadia

∽ ∽ ∽

Dear Kids,

I've just finished reading the letters you wrote to me last month. They are really amazing letters. I wonder if you have any idea how special you all are. I get a lot of mail about *Tuck Everlasting,* and I'm proud to get it, but—well, I don't often see letters so beautifully written, so clearly expressed, and as thoughtful as yours.

I wish I had time to answer each and every one of your questions, but of course I don't, and it probably isn't fair to single out just one particular question, but I'm going to do it anyway. One of you said, ". . . why did Winnie pour the spring water on the toad. If she did not want to disturb her wheel of life, why did she disturb the toad's?" This was especially interesting to me because a boy in California wrote much the same question a couple of years ago, and we got into a fascinating discussion (by mail) about whether or not animals are aware of mortality. I said no, he said yes. And he believed that the toad was out in the middle of the road in the Epilogue because it was hoping that somehow it would get killed, whereas I meant to imply that the toad, being a creature with next to no intelligence, was out there because it didn't know any better. So, one of these days, when you all and Mrs. Waltz have time, you might have a debate about animal awareness, and let me know how it comes out.

Now about this business of a sequel. I will never write a sequel to *Tuck*. There are several reasons why not, but one of them certainly is that sequels, unless they're planned on from the beginning, are almost never as good as the first story they try to continue. I've been disappointed many times by unjustified sequels. To write a sequel just because you think it'll sell well—bad idea. Some of you said that you'd like to know what happened to the Tucks after they left Treegap, but you see, that's just the point—nothing happened. I have thought for a long time that it would be sad and lonely to live forever, but I also think it would be boring. What *could* happen? One of the things that keeps life exciting and meaningful is exactly the fact that we know we don't have forever. As for Winnie, she lived a normal life, I'm sure, and that means that not much happened to her, either. Not much has happened to *me*. Most of us lead pretty quiet lives. I have had a very lucky, happy life, but you couldn't make a novel out of it. So—no sequel. Some of you may want lives that are full of adventures, and if that's so, I hope you will be able to arrange things that way, but for most of us—well, in case you haven't read another story of mine called *Knee·knock Rise*, there's a character in that story who says, "sheep and bread and flat fields—that's what the days are."

Now it's time to stop all this and pass along my recipe. It's a good thing you like my stories because you wouldn't like my cooking very much. I don't even like my cooking. But we have to eat! The recipe I'm sending wasn't invented by me: I got it from one of my nieces. But it's a good one that I used all the time.

I wish I could come to your school and visit you, but that isn't going to happen. So I'll just end by saying that I know you'll go on eating, but I hope you'll go on reading, too, and I wish you a chain of teachers as good as Mrs. Waltz clearly is.

My very best to you all.

Your friend,
Natalie Babbitt

P.S. I'm enclosing an explanation of how the ash tree and the spring in *Tuck* were destroyed. It seems to me a few of you asked about that.

How the Tree in Tuck Everlasting *Was Destroyed . . .*

The tree in the center of the Fosters' wood is an ash tree. It is modeled on the great ash tree, *Yggdrasil* (no, I don't know how to pronounce it, either), which was the king of trees in an ancient Norwegian tree religion. Yggdrasil had three rivers flowing at its base, one of which was the River of Life. In *Tuck Everlasting* I gave the ash tree a spring that held the water of life, rather than a river, but the effect is the same.

The idea of water as the giver and preserver of life is very common in ancient religions. I think the cavemen must have realized pretty early that they had to have water to survive, and anything that was necessary came to have great religious importance. This idea lasted for a long time.

You have read about Ponce de Leon who came to this continent almost 500 years ago, looking for the Fountain of Youth, and instead discovered Florida.

That was long after the start of Christianity, of course, but a lot of bits and pieces of ancient religions stayed active and are still active today. Many Christians put up Christmas trees at holiday time, but there is nothing about Christmas trees in the Bible. They are survivors of an old pre-Christian winter festival and we seem to have hung on to them because we like them so much. Another good example is church bells. We think of them now as being there to call people to Sunday services, but originally they were put there because people believed that bells would scare away the Devil.

Anyway, on page 41 in the book, Jesse Tuck tells Winnie Foster that Pa Tuck thinks the tree and the spring are "something left over from—well, from some other plan for the way the world should be. Some plan that didn't work out too good. And so everything was changed. Except that the spring was passed over, somehow or other." From this you are supposed to understand that, by "some other plan," Pa Tuck meant some other, older religion.

About 75 years ago, in the 1920s, a group of Christian monks in northern England went out to a hilltop where there was a grove of ash trees, and they chopped them all down. They did this, as they explained it, to put an end, once and for all, to that old tree religion, which had spread to England from Norway centuries before. But there are no monks in *Tuck Everlasting.* Instead, the ash tree and the spring are destroyed by lightning.

Lightning is another of those things in nature that, like water, were once believed to have religious importance. In Greek and Roman religions, for instance, lightning was thought to be a weapon used by the gods. If you've seen Disney's movie *Fantasia,* you will remember the scene where, in a rainstorm, the clouds part and Zeus, the chief Greek god, throws lightning bolts at the little half-horse-half-human creatures, called centaurs, that have been playing together down on Earth. Lightning as a weapon is an idea that has hung on for a long time. You may have heard some grown-up say, "May lightning strike me dead if I'm not telling the truth," and they don't mean lightning sent by Zeus. They mean lightning sent by God—whatever God they may believe in, but mainly the Christian-Judaic God.

So—if you put all these things together, what you are meant to understand is that the ash tree and the spring in *Tuck Everlasting* are part of an ancient religion that somehow survived into modern times, and that when the Christian-Judaic God, looking down one day, noticed them at last, He sent a lightning bolt to destroy them—because we all know a god can do anything.

I didn't put all this stuff into the story because, as you can see, it takes a long time to explain, and anyway I thought everyone would understand about the lightning. But I was wrong. Lots and lots of readers have been confused by the tree's destruction, and that is my fault, though I'm not sure how to correct the situation. So I have learned something: Never put into a story something that is going to confuse readers. And you have learned something, too—about ash trees and magic springs and lightning. So maybe we're even.

Recipe from Natalie Babbitt . . .

Vegetable and Cracker Dip

Cooking Equipment:
    Small mixing bowl
    Metal spoon

Cutting knife
Cutting board

Ingredients:
8 ounces sour cream
2 or 3 foil packets of George Washington's Golden Seasoning and Broth
Carrots, cut into sticks
Celery, cut into sticks

Preparation:
1. Mix sour cream and seasoning in a small mixing bowl.
2. Serve chilled with carrot and celery sticks on the side of bowl.

SERVES 2–4

Author's Remarks:
Boxes of seasoning are small and contain 8 packets. You can also serve this dip with crackers or potato chips.

ᴥ ᴥ ᴥ ᴥ ᴥ

Francisco Jiménez

Dear Francisco Jiménez,

Hello, my name is Kevin. I am a fairly good reader and I like to use my skills as a reader, not just for school but also for pleasure reading. It just happens in school we were reading one of your stories, titled "The Circuit." I like this story because it showed what life was like for migrant workers and you described it in full detail. You explained how it was hard by saying how they moved so often. That is why I liked your story.

As a sixth grader I don't have an acquired taste for many vegetables, but I do like foods such as pizza, steak, and other things like chicken. I think that having a favorite food is important; you can look forward to something that your mother or grandmother makes every few months. My favorite food is rib eye steak marinated in Montreal Steak Seasoning, cooked medium. I am asking you to please send me your favorite recipe, such as a grandmother's secret recipe or a family recipe . . .

Kevin Atieh

Dear Francisco Jiménez,

I am twelve years old and I love to play baseball. I also enjoy learning about different cultures. In our class we are writing to authors whose works we enjoy reading about the most. When my teacher asked us to pick a favorite author, your short story, "The Circuit," really stood out. I picked your fabulous story because I learned so many interesting facts about it. It also was fun learning about different kinds of lifestyles. I understand that you went through the same lifestyle as the boy in the story called Panchito, and you write your stories based on your family's past. It must have been painful moving every couple of months. Two kids in class won a contest writing a poem about you, as a migrant child worker.

We are doing this fabulous project in reading and *we need your help . . .*

Chris Lee

∾ ∾ ∾

Dear Kevin and Chris,

You cannot imagine how pleased I was to receive your letters and to know that you have chosen me as one of your favorite authors. I feel honored.

Your class project of putting together a unique cookbook of authors and their favorite recipes to raise money for a children's literary foundation is a wonderful and inspirational idea. Please thank your teacher for encouraging such a worthwhile project.

One of my favorite recipes is Salsa Ranchera. Good luck on your project and thank you both for writing to me.

Sincerely yours,
Francisco Jiménez

Recipe from Francisco Jiménez . . .

Salsa Ranchera

Cooking Equipment:
   Cutting knife
   Cutting board
   Small saucepan
   Measuring cup
   Measuring spoons
   Wooden spoon

Ingredients:
   3 tomatoes
   ¼ cup water or less
   ½ onion, chopped
   2 garlic cloves, chopped
   2–3 Serrano peppers, chopped
   1 teaspoon cooking oil
   Juice of ½ lemon
   1 teaspoon oregano

Preparation:
   1. Cut tomatoes into quarters, remove core, and cook in water in a small saucepan over low heat until soft.

2. Gently mash tomatoes into pieces and set aside to cool.
3. Stir together tomatoes and chopped ingredients, then add oil, lemon juice, and oregano to taste.
4. Serve chilled or at room temperature.

SERVES 2–4

∿ ∿ ∿ ∿ ∿

Megan Whalen Turner

Dear Megan Whalen Turner,

Wazzup! My name is Amanda and I live in New Jersey. I am twelve years old and was born in Coral Springs, Florida. I have two brothers and they are the most annoying people you will ever meet (which I hope you never would!).

The literary device that I look for in books is foreshadowing. No matter how hard I try I never really find a book on the kind of foreshadowing as you used in your book, *The Thief*. It contained the best examples of foreshadowing that I have ever read! I just kept on reading and reading! I mean it. No matter how hard I try I just couldn't stop reading your book. I am going to read the sequel, *The Queen of Attolia*. The only reason why I would is because of the suspense that was in *The Thief*.

The only obsession I had in your book was when you couldn't make the ending have more action. In other words, (no offense) you lacked somewhat of action. I want it to be like *bam!* Or *boom!* Which you kind of had some of. No matter what I think of the ending, *The Thief* was the best book in the world. It was brilliant! I can image everything you wrote about. The setting, the characters, the mood that they were in. It was amazing. I mean it. I'm already repeating my words!

Furthermore, I would like to ask you so many questions that I hope you answer all for me! Question number one, *where do you get the names for the characters?* I was so into the book that I had to know how to say the names! Which I did. And you have the most excellent names for your characters. Especially Eugenides. Since you described the characters too much I knew their names from the start! Question number two, *did you go to the maze and find the stone?* I mean OMG! (It means Oh My Gosh!) You explained the maze so well that I'm in the maze when you are describing it . . .

Amanda Meinwieser

∿ ∿ ∿

Dear Amanda,

It's hard for me to believe that it's been ten months since you wrote your letter to me. I am sorry that it has taken me so long to respond. I enjoyed your letter. It was very exciting. It's a neat thing for an author to get mail from individuals and to realize how many different kinds of people from very different backgrounds like my book. I have mail from people in the United States and Britain and I just got a letter last week from Japan. I would never have guessed that people all over the world would read *The Thief*.

Some answers to your questions. Many of the names in the book are Greek or are based on Greek names. I am sure you have heard the name "Eugene." I didn't make Eugenides out of Eugene. I actually dug up the root word I was looking for, one to characterize a fortuitous birth, and then turned it into a name. Then I realized that someone long ago must have done the same thing with the name "Eugene." Many of the names we use today have Greek origins. There was an Alexander twenty-five hundred years ago, Alexander the Great. He created an enormous empire around the Mediterranean. His father's name was Philip. I find it a little mind boggling to think of thousands and thousands of years of "Philips" in history.

The maze that I describe I mostly made up, but I did get the idea from a real experience I had in Greece when I went down a narrow stairwell carved in solid rock to get to an underground cistern. I remembered the shape of the walls and the carving and incorporated those in my description.

I am afraid it is too late to send a recipe, but if you still want one you can let me know. Thanks for writing.

Very truly yours,
Megan Whalen Turner

P.S. I have two older brothers myself—and an older sister. The older they get, the better.

Recipe from Megan Whalen Turner . . .

Walnut Pesto

Cooking Equipment:
Food processor
Measuring cup
Cheese grater
Small bowl
Heavy frying pan
Wooden spoon

Ingredients:
3 cups or one generously sized fresh bunch of basil leaves
½ cup Parmesan cheese
½ cup walnuts
1 garlic clove
Olive oil

Preparation:
1. Remove stems from basil leaves. Place washed and dried leaves into food processor and chop very fine.
2. In a small bowl grate Parmesan cheese finely and add to basil leaves. I like to use the large holes on the cheese grater and have a coarser pesto.

3. Place walnuts in a frying pan over medium heat and stir occasionally until pan is hot, then turn heat off.
4. Place cooled walnuts and garlic clove into food processor and blend.
5. While the food processor is running, open the spout at the top of the lid and dribble in enough oil to turn pesto into a paste.

YIELDS 1–1½ CUPS

Author's Remarks:

By stirring occasionally you might get the first batch of walnuts toasted without burning them. If not, try again with more walnuts. I've been burning the first batch for years.

You can put the pesto on pasta, chicken, or fish. Just add it to the hot food and it melts a little. I like to spread it on French bread with a soft goat cheese and eat it as an hors d'oeuvre.

2 ❧ Breads

Jean Craighead George

Dear Jean Craighead George,

Hi. I am a sixth-grade student attending middle school. I am very busy with after school activities. I usually do my homework late then go right to bed, so I barely ever get a chance to read. When I do get to read I prefer one of your books.

My favorite book of yours is *On the Far Side of the Mountain*. I love survivor type of books because they are neat. I especially love when the main character has a wild animal friend. I always wished I could live in the woods. When I was like 4 or 5 I would pretend my room was the woods and all my stuffed animals were wild animals that I became friends with and I could talk to them. I obviously never did live in the woods, but your books were as close as I could get. You are an amazing author and that is why *I love* your books.

In my reading class we are working on making a book . . .

Krista Mahalchik

∾ ∾ ∾

Dear Krista,

My son Luke brought this recipe home the year our garden produced so many zucchinis, we needed all the recipes we could get to keep ahead of them. This is the best.

I hope this letter and recipe arrive in time.

Sincerely,
Jean Craighead George

Recipe from Jean Craighead George . . .

Zucchini Walnut Bread

Cooking Equipment:
> 2 9×5-inch loaf pans
> Grater
> Eggbeater or electric mixer
> Large mixing bowl
> Measuring cups
> Measuring spoons
> Wooden spoon

Ingredients:
> 2 cups grated zucchini
> 4 eggs

2 cups sugar
1 cup vegetable oil
3½ cups flour
¾ teaspoon baking powder
1½ teaspoons baking soda
1 teaspoon cinnamon
1 cup walnuts
1 cup raisins
1 teaspoon vanilla

Preparation:
1. Move oven rack to lowest position.
2. Preheat oven to 350°.
3. Grease and flour loaf pans.
4. Beat eggs in large mixing bowl, then stir in sugar and oil.
5. Stir in flour, baking powder, baking soda, cinnamon, and grated zucchini.
6. Stir in walnuts, raisins, and vanilla.
7. Pour into greased pans and bake for 55–75 minutes.

MAKES 2 LOAVES

ෆ ෆ ෆ ෆ ෆ

Roy MacGregor

Dear Roy MacGregor,

Hello, my name is Greg and I have read many of your books. The reason I love your books is because I read in your biography that you are a big hockey fan. I know you especially enjoy writing books. I personally like hockey and my goal is to be a professional hockey player. I especially love reading your books. I'm amazed at how you create a book about your favorite sport and turn it into a mystery.

My personal favorite from your *Screech Owls* series is *Mystery at Lake Placid*. This was my favorite because I've actually played hockey in Lake Placid. Your books made me feel like I was actually playing the game when the players started skating down the ice. I could also feel what it was like when one of the characters had to go in the locker room that was pitch black and he was trying to find the person who was stealing the team's hockey equipment.

I think you're a great author because you write with detail and therefore I know exactly what you're talking about, like when you're describing the players skating around the rink. I'm very happy there is an author who enjoys the same activities and hobbies that I do . . .

Greg Zambon

ෆ ෆ ෆ

Hi Greg,

I sure am delighted to hear you like the *Screech Owls*—all the gang says "Hi!"—but can't say as I'm particularly pleased to be asked about my cooking. I find peanut butter on toast complicated—as the joking and kidding of my four kids attest to. I once boiled water all by myself to make a cup of instant coffee. I can, however, feed myself, so long as Ellen cuts the meat into small chunks and they spray me down with a hose every so often. My mother-in-law, Rose, made the most wonderful banana nut bread. I do not know where the recipe came from, though it did come from her farm in Saskatchewan at some point. Ellen uses this recipe and I have stolen it from her when she wasn't looking. Good luck with your project.

Roy MacGregor

Recipe from Roy MacGregor . . .

Banana Nut Bread

Cooking Equipment:
9 × 5-inch loaf pan
Large mixing bowl
Flour sifter
Measuring cups
Measuring spoons
Wooden spoon

Ingredients:
2 cups flour
1 teaspoon baking soda
2 teaspoons baking powder
¾ teaspoon salt
½ cup shortening
2 eggs, beaten
1 cup sugar
1 cup mashed bananas (2–3 bananas)
½ cup or ¾ cup chopped walnuts

Preparation:
1. Preheat oven to 350°.
2. Grease and flour loaf pan.
3. In a large mixing bowl sift flour, baking soda, and baking powder, then add salt.
4. Blend in shortening, beaten eggs, and sugar.
5. Stir in mashed bananas and walnuts.
6. Mix all ingredients well, spoon into pan, and bake for 60–75 minutes.

MAKES 1 LOAF

Valerie Tripp

Dear Valerie Tripp,

My name is Ashley. I am in the sixth grade and I love the books that you write!!! I love *Molly's Surprise*. It was really a nice book. My favorite part in the book is when Molly and her brothers get to open their presents and they each get something they want. Molly got a doll that was dressed like a nurse. I like the Molly book from the *American Girls* series because I like a book about girls from history, I like to know more about how they lived. I think you are a good author and you really get your mind into the book like you were really that girl. That is what I think is unique about you. I don't really like to read all the time, sometimes I read to my next-door neighbor to help her read. She is in the third grade. I have two American girl dolls, Molly and Felicity; I also am collecting them . . .

Ashley Hyman

∾ ∾ ∾

Dear Ashley,

Thank you very much for your lovely letter. I am glad that you like the books, especially *Molly's Surprise*!! It is always a pleasure to hear from a wonderful friend of the *American Girls* like you!

I am enclosing a biography that has pictures and information about my childhood. It answers many of the questions my readers ask me, including the question I am asked most frequently. That question is: Where do the ideas for the stories come from? The answer is: The ideas come from historical research, memories of my own childhood, my experiences and observations, my imagination, and also from suggestions from my readers just like you. Many readers ask: Do I have a pet: And the answer is, yes! We have a big, gentle, golden retriever named Sunday. If you asked other questions, I answered them by writing on your letter.

Your cookbook sounds wonderful, Ashley! I would be honored, pleased and delighted to have my recipe included. I had to think a long while before I chose one recipe as a favorite. I like to cook and to experiment. It's fun to play around with recipes and add a little of this, a little less of that, and substitute a pinch of whatsis for something—or—other.

I hope you have a wonderful year and that you continue to read and to use your imagination all your life long! Thank you for writing to me!

Your friend,
Valerie Tripp

P.S. I love your illustrations of Katharine, Molly's nurse doll.
P.P.S. Yes, I am coming out with new books next month.

Recipe from Valerie Tripp . . .

Quick Sweet Whole Wheat Bread

Cooking Equipment:
> 9 × 5-inch loaf pan
> Large mixing bowl
> Small mixing bowl
> Measuring cups
> Measuring spoons
> Wooden spoon

Ingredients:
> Butter for greasing pan
> $2\frac{1}{2}$ cups whole wheat flour
> $\frac{1}{2}$ teaspoon cinnamon
> $\frac{1}{4}$ teaspoon salt
> 1 teaspoon baking soda
> 1 egg, beaten
> $\frac{1}{2}$ cup molasses
> $\frac{1}{4}$ cup brown sugar
> $\frac{1}{4}$ cup sesame, peanut, or sunflower oil
> 1 teaspoon grated lemon or orange peel
> $\frac{2}{3}$ cup plain yogurt

Preparation:
1. Preheat oven to 375°.
2. Grease loaf pan with butter.
3. Mix whole wheat flour, cinnamon, salt, and baking soda together in large mixing bowl and set aside.
4. Combine beaten egg, molasses, brown sugar, oil, and grated peel in small mixing bowl.
5. Add plain yogurt to egg mixture and then alternately add it to the dry ingredients.
6. Pour batter into loaf pan and bake for 50 minutes.

MAKES 1 LOAF

Author's Remarks:
Have all the ingredients at room temperature. This recipe for bread is easy. Your whole house smells wonderful as it bakes. Molly's mother or Mrs. Guilford might have used it because it has no white sugar.

3 ⦿ Breakfast Foods

Frank Asch

Dear Frank Asch,

I have read your awesome poetry book called *Sawgrass Poems: A View of the Everglades.* I thoroughly enjoyed it.

We are doing a project for a children's literacy foundation. We want to make a cookbook of authors' favorite recipes. I am asking you if you can send me your favorite recipe. It can be anything, as long as it's edible . . .

Heidi

∾ ∾ ∾

Dear Heidi,

My favorite recipe is "Mooncake." My favorite line is: "That's okay I forgive you!"

Love,
Frank Asch

Recipe from Frank Asch . . .

Mooncake

Cooking Equipment:
Small mixing bowl
Eggbeater or whisk
Measuring cup
Metal spoon
Omelet pan
Cooking spatula

Ingredients:
2 eggs
A pinch of salt
¼ cup of Grape Nuts cereal
Maple syrup
Fresh fruit, sliced or in bite-sized chunks

Preparation:
1. Beat eggs with a pinch of salt.
2. Stir in Grape Nuts and fry like a pancake in omelet pan.
3. Remove pancake when cooked and top with syrup and fruit.

SERVES 1–2

Author's Remarks:
    Mmmmm!

❧ ❧ ❧ ❧ ❧

Edward Bloor

Dear Edward Bloor,

I am a sixth-grade twelve-year-old girl who has great parents along with my bothersome younger sister. I have two hamsters, Shelly and Junior.

I used to hate reading books but now I love them. I can't believe I used to hate reading them! I have enjoyed your first novel, *Tangerine*. It is a remarkable book and I hope that you will write more books similar to it for us young kids. My favorite part of this novel was when Paul's parents found out the truth about his brother. He was doing so many harmful things that I wished someone would do something about it. Paul's parent's thought that Paul was at fault for his brother's crime. This made me feel so bad for Paul.

Tangerine is an astonishing book because it has so much thrill put into it. At times it will make you feel like you are placed into Paul's position, facing all his brother's dangers. I'm glad that you made Paul brave and through all his strength he was able to face it all to the end.

I know that this was your first novel. I did some research and correct me if I'm wrong, but I have found out that you used to teach both middle and high school in Florida. I found out that you have a wife and children, and that you have a miniature poodle named Zak. I also know that you have written another wonderful book called *Crusader* . . .

Sabina Della-Peruta

❧ ❧ ❧

Dear Sabina,

Thank you for your letter about *Tangerine* and for adding that lovely border art. My second novel, *Crusader,* is now out in a big, fat paperback from Scholastic. I just finished my third novel this week. It's titled *Story Time.* It's about a haunted library. It should be out in hardcover from Harcourt in the spring of 2004. [Now published.]

You seem to have learned many facts about me from research. I must update my dog situation, though: The poodle, Zak, has now been joined by a black Pomeranian-mix named Chloe.

I certainly do want to support Mrs. Waltz's project in behalf of the Children's Literacy Foundation. I have enclosed a recipe of my mother's. She grew up in the Pennsylvania coal mines. Shoo-fly Pie is one of the recipes she brought from there. It remains a family favorite of ours because you can eat it for dessert or for breakfast.

Yours sincerely,
Edward Bloor

Recipe from Edward Bloor . . .

Shoo-fly Pie

Cooking Equipment:
Large mixing bowl
Measuring cups
Measuring spoons
Wooden spoon

Ingredients:

FLOUR MIXTURE:
1½ cups sifted flour
½ cup Crisco
½ cup brown sugar
¼ teaspoon salt
¼ teaspoon cinnamon
Unbaked pie shell (hold for later)

LIQUID MIXTURE:
½ teaspoon baking soda
½ cup baking molasses (Brer Rabbit Light)
½ cup hot water

Preparation:
1. Preheat oven to 350°.
2. Combine flour, Crisco, brown sugar, and salt to make flour mixture; then take ¼ cup of mixture, add cinnamon to it, and set aside for top of pie.
3. Dissolve baking soda with baking molasses and hot water. Mix well.
4. Add liquid mixture to remaining flour mixture.
5. Put in unbaked pie shell.
6. Cover with topping mixture and bake for 45 minutes.

SERVES 4–6

Rob Childs

Dear Rob Childs,

Hello my name is Duncan. I live in the U.S. I love all your books and you are my favourite author. I have read all your books because all of my family are English and we visit England quite often (Hull and Manchester). I especially like the *Football Mad* series about Luke Crawford and the

Swillsby Swifts, particularly *All Goalies Are Crazy* and *Football Daft.* I like them both very much. This series is always about Luke thinking he is good and playing worse and Sanjay making fun of Tubs. They are hysterical. Your books taught me about sportsmanship and teamwork. I would like to say, "Keep on writing."

Duncan Swanwick

∾ ∾ ∾

Dear Duncan,

Thanks very much for your letter, Duncan. It's always good to hear from youngsters who have enjoyed reading my books and taken the trouble to write me about them. It's the first time, though, that I've ever been asked for a recipe!

Please feel free to include the enclosed recipe in your planned book for one of my favorite meals, Sausage Pie. I enjoy cooking whenever I get the chance, and always love eating sausages!

By the way, if you do write to me again about anything, please do so via Transworld in London. I'm afraid your letter was sent to the wrong address in Leicester, much to the surprise of a certain Bob Childs who lives there!

Delighted to learn how much you like the *Soccer Mad* series about Luke Crawford and his bunch of Sunday soccer misfits. The latest tale, *Soccer Shocks,* shows what happens to the Swifts at the end of the season. I've really enjoyed writing about the efforts of characters like Luke, Sanjay, Tubs, and the rest. By the way, did you know that the first two stories in the series are also available on cassette tape, read by actor Tom Watt?

Hope you like playing the game yourself, Duncan. I know soccer is becoming more and more popular in the States. I was a crazy goalie myself at school like Sanjay, which must be the reason why so many of my stories feature goalies as the main characters. It's a very dramatic position, crucial to the success of the team. The keeper is often the hero or the villain, making vital saves or costly mistakes.

Thanks again for writing me, Duncan. I'm also enclosing a biography sheet that gives you more information about myself and my writing, plus personal bookmarks and designed book covers that might look good on some display somewhere for a while.

Best wishes!

Yours sincerely,
Rob Childs

Recipe from Rob Childs . . .

Sausage and Potato Pie

Cooking Equipment:
Large frying pan
Cutting knife

Cutting board
Small mixing bowl
Large mixing bowl
Saucepan
Potato masher
Wooden spoon
Deep pie pan or 8-inch square pan
Rubber spatula

Ingredients:

12 ounces or more sausages
2 onions, sliced
4 ounces sliced mushrooms
2 tablespoons margarine
2 tablespoons flour
$\frac{1}{2}$ cup milk
$\frac{1}{2}$ cup beef stock
1 pound of mashed potatoes
$\frac{1}{2}$ cup grated cheddar cheese
2 tablespoons butter
$\frac{1}{4}$ cup milk or less
1 teaspoon French mustard

Preparation:

1. Preheat oven to 400° or Gas Mark 6.
2. Cook sausages in frying pan, cool, cut into wheels, and set aside.
3. Fry sliced onions and mushrooms in margarine until tender.
4. Mix flour, milk, and beef stock in small bowl.
5. Pour over fried onions and mushrooms and bring to a boil while stirring for about a minute.
6. Stir in and heat cooked sausages and French mustard.
7. Turn sausage mixture into a deep pie pan.
8. Peel, boil, and mash potatoes.
9. Blend cheddar cheese, butter, and milk with mashed potatoes in large bowl.
10. Spread potato mixture over sausages using spatula and bake for 15–20 minutes.

SERVES 4–6

Author's Remarks:

Serve with a selection of vegetables—and enjoy!

Norton Juster

Dear Norton Juster,

I want to start out by saying I liked your novel *The Phantom Tollbooth*. I have read it four times. I like it because it is so creative and adventurous. It has so many different characters. I don't normally read a lot of books but this one really appealed to me. I simply love your book . . .

Alissa Mirchuk

∾ ∾ ∾

Dear Alissa,

Thanks for your nice letter. I'm a waffle freak, so here's a good waffle recipe.

Have fun,
Norton Juster

Recipe from Norton Juster . . .

Buttermilk Waffles

Cooking Equipment:
2 large bowls
Small bowl
Whisk or electric mixer
Measuring cups
Measuring spoons
Wooden spoon
Waffle maker

Ingredients:
1½ cups unbleached all-purpose flour
½ cup whole wheat flour
1 teaspoon baking soda
½ teaspoon baking powder
¼ teaspoon salt
Pinch of cinnamon
4 eggs, separated
¼ cup vegetable oil
2 cups buttermilk

Preparation:
1. Preheat waffle maker.
2. Combine flours, baking soda, baking powder, salt, and cinnamon in a large bowl and set aside.
3. Beat egg yokes, oil, and buttermilk in a large bowl until foamy.

4. Add egg mixture to dry ingredients and mix until moistened.
5. Beat egg whites in small bowl until fluffy and soft peaks form.
6. Fold egg whites into mixture until no streaks are visible.
7. If necessary, brush the waffle iron grids with oil or melted butter.
8. Pour about ½ cup of batter onto waffle maker grid, close lid, and cook for 4 minutes until done.
9. Remove and serve hot.

SERVES 6–8

Author's Remarks:

Eat them with syrup, confectioners' sugar, or anything else you like on them. If you want, you can add blueberries, chopped nuts, or chocolate chips to the mix.

∾ ∾ ∾ ∾ ∾

Theodore Taylor

Dear Theodore Taylor,

I love your book *The Cay.* I completely understand what you're trying to say. I think prejudice should stop, and people should treat each other equally. *The Cay* is my favorite book and is a great story . . .

Anthony Gelormini

Dear Theodore Taylor,

My name is Matt and I am a sixth-grade student who loves to read. After reading your book *The Cay,* I was very impressed. Not only was it a great book, but also it gave me a whole different view on racism. At each part in the book I felt I was there because of your great descriptions. In addition to this, I would like to compliment you on many things.

You described the setting beautifully. Your theme of the book, which was about racism, was done in a very original way. I really like the part when Philip went blind, because it showed how a person's color really doesn't matter at all. There were parts in the book that were very tense and suspenseful, such as when there was the storm and when Timothy died . . .

Matthew Glassman

∿ ∿ ∿

Dear Anthony and Matt,

Thank you for your letters and I'm so glad you enjoyed *The Cay*. I'm enclosing some information about the writings of that book and the prequel-sequel, *Timothy of the Cay*. I've sent my recipe to Mrs. Waltz, Egg Pie.

Hope you'll try it.

Sincerely,
Theodore Taylor

Recipe from Theodore Taylor . . .

Egg Pie

Cooking Equipment:
Cutting knife
Iron frying pan (jumbo size)
Wooden spoon
Eggbeater or fork
13 × 9 × 2-inch baking dish

Ingredients:
6 bacon strips
1 onion, diced
1 can peeled tomatoes (28 ounces)
1 can sliced mushrooms, drained (2½ ounces)
2 cans Vienna sausages (5 ounces), drained and cut into wheels,
    ¼-inch thick
Pimiento strips
1 dozen eggs, beaten
½ cup milk
6 slices Jack or American cheese
Parmesan cheese

Preparation:

1. Preheat oven to 350°.
2. Cut bacon strips into 1-inch pieces.
3. Fry bacon in frying pan until crisp, pour off most of grease, and brown diced onions in the remaining grease.
4. Stir in tomatoes, mushrooms, Vienna sausages, and pimiento strips and simmer for 15 minutes.
5. Add beaten eggs and milk and stir gently.
6. Add cheese slices during last few minutes.
7. Carefully pour mixture into baking dish and bake for 30 minutes until eggs have a nice golden crust.
8. Sprinkle Parmesan cheese over crust during the last 5 minutes.

SERVES 12

∾ ∾ ∾ ∾ ∾

4 ❧ Soups and Sandwiches

Judy Blume

Dear Judy Blume,

Your books have really encouraged me to read because you are the reason that I enjoy reading. The books you write have a very enthusiastic opening and they pull the reader right into the story and you don't want to put the book down!

I especially enjoyed *Blubber*! I read it when I was in the fifth grade, and went to Borders that weekend and purchased it because I loved it so much! I have read it over ten times and am still reading it . . .

Amanda Brody

∿ ∿ ∿

Dear Amanda and Friends,

During the summer of 1980 I spent a month in Maine, on a small island off Port Clyde. Twice a week we grocery shopped by boat and always stopped for lunch at a tiny sandwich shop. That's where I first tasted broccoli salad. By the end of the month I convinced the owner of the shop to tell me her secret, which I'm happy to share with you. It's delicious, healthy, and tastes a lot better than it sounds (as long as you like broccoli). It can be made from fresh uncooked or lightly steamed broccoli.

Love,
Judy Blume

Recipe from Judy Blume . . .

Port Clyde Broccoli Salad Sandwich

Cooking Equipment:
Cutting knife
Cutting board
Small mixing bowl
Metal spoon

Ingredients:
Broccoli
Mayonnaise
Juice from a lemon wedge
Salt and pepper to taste

Preparation:
1. Chop broccoli florets into tiny pieces.
2. Add just enough mayonnaise to keep the salad together.

3. Squeeze in the juice from a wedge of lemon.
4. Add salt and pepper to taste. Mix well.
5. Spread on your favorite kind of bread.

SERVES 2–4

Author's Remarks:
    Yum!

☙ ☙ ☙ ☙ ☙

Karen Cushman

Dear Karen Cushman,

    I enjoyed reading one of your books and I look forward to being entertained by more. This book that I discovered was very humorous was *Catherine, Called Birdy*. In this book you discuss the hard life of Catherine, who is called Birdy, and some of her issues.

    In my research I have found that you originally wanted to ". . . dig for treasures on the Acropolis by moonlight," and also that you make up your stories the hard way, by using extensive research. But I am delighted with your writings and some of the information that I came across about you; like that you came from an ethnic working class Chicago family.

    I want to thank you for reading my letter and being a great author. But I mostly want to thank you for making your books what they are so that I'm not bored out of my mind, falling asleep in front of a textbook. But instead, I'm cracking up with everyone staring at me and wondering why I'm laughing . . .

Leeann Eula

☙ ☙ ☙

Dear Leeann,

    Thanks for your very thoughtful letter. Your recipe book sounds like a fun project and I am happy to contribute.

    It was hard for me to find a recipe to send because after all these years (and years and years and years) of cooking, I don't really use recipes anymore. I look and see what is in the cupboard and the refrigerator and then figure out an interesting way to put it all together. But I do like this soup because I love chips and cheese—especially together.

    Now don't get so busy cooking that you forget to read!

All my best,
Karen Cushman

Dear Karen Cushman,

    In reading class our class split into two groups. One side read *Catherine, Called Birdy* and the other side read *The Midwife's Apprentice*. I read *The Midwife's Apprentice*.

I would just like to compliment you on how excellent your book was. Personally, I really liked it. It had a really good meaning to it, and the story line was very good. It had many cliffhangers, which made me want to keep reading on and I didn't want to put the book down. My favorite part of the story was when Alyce saved the boy when he was drowning and she saved the cat from the eel.

I also liked the ending when Alyce decided to be an apprentice again, and how the midwife wouldn't let her help unless she said that she would not give up and she would try, etc.

The ending, I thought, was the best part of the book, and the most meaningful. I am going to try to read some of your other books and see if they are as good as *The Midwife's Apprentice* . . .

Emily Zoellner

Dear Karen Cushman,

My name is Lindsay. I am in sixth grade and in reading class we just recently finished reading your novel *The Midwife's Apprentice*. I loved it! Personally, I think that it was the best book I have read in the last three years! I have read that *The Midwife's Apprentice* is your favorite book out of the two that you have written.

My favorite character was the cat. From the picture on the cover and the way I picture him, and the way I imagined he acts, Purr reminds me of my cat Duke. They seem to look a lot alike.

One of my favorite parts of the book was when you said that they had changed the name of the inn to "The Cat and Cheese."

A couple of days ago, I checked out *Catherine, Called Birdy* from the library. I have just started to read it, however, my sister has read it and she says that it is one of the best books she has ever read.

At this point in the story, which is only chapter two, I already like it. I cannot wait to finish my homework each day so that I can read a couple of pages . . .

Lindsay Abken

Dear Karen Cushman,

My name is Scott. I am a sixth-grade student and attend middle school. I have two sisters that like to read. I also like to read. Your book *Catherine, Called Birdy* was one of the best books I have ever read. I enjoyed the part when Catherine ran away the most because it was a new adventure in the book that I didn't expect to happen. The book taught me about the ways of people who lived in the Middle Ages. The different problems Birdy had made the story exciting . . .

Scott Graff

∾ ∾ ∾

Dear Emily, Lindsay, and Scott,

I am very pleased to participate in your cookbook project. I was contacted by several of your classmates and sent my recipe in already.

Good luck with the book—let me know how everything tastes.

Sincerely,
Karen Cushman

Recipe from Karen Cushman . . .

Tortilla Soup

Cooking Equipment:
Cutting knife
Cutting board
Measuring cups
Measuring spoons
Large pot
Ladle

Ingredients:
¼ cup onions, chopped
¼ cup green pepper, chopped
2 cloves garlic, chopped
1 tablespoon or so oil
6 cups chicken broth
8-ounce can of chopped green chilies
4 fresh tomatoes (or equivalent canned), chopped
1 teaspoon ground cumin
2 cups chicken, cut into small pieces
Corn cut from one ear (or equivalent frozen)
¼ cup or so chopped cilantro
Tortilla chips
1–1½ cups of shredded cheese (Jack or cheddar)

Preparation:
1. Sauté onions, green pepper, and garlic in oil until soft.
2. Add broth, chilies, tomatoes, and cumin and simmer for
   20 minutes.
3. Stir in raw chicken and corn and simmer for 25 minutes more.
4. Add cilantro just before serving.
5. Ladle soup into large bowls.
6. Top with crumbled tortilla chips and shredded cheese.

SERVES 4–6

Author's Remarks:
You can use cooked chicken instead. Add it at the end and simmer just to heat.

෨ ෨ ෨ ෨ ෨

Carol Gorman

Dear Carol Gorman,

Hello, my name is Marly and I'm a big fan of your writing. I read your first book, *The Miraculous Makeover of Lizard Flanagan,* when I was in the fourth grade. I realized that you had written many more books so I found those and read them too. Many of your books deal with real life and what happens when kids are changing the most. I like the part in *The Miraculous Makeover* when Lizard came to school only to find that everything was different, and all her friends had changed into these boy crazy girls (just like at my school).

Also, I liked reading the part when Lizard went shopping, bought a skirt, and liked it. Lizard and Mary Ann were best friends and nothing could come between them. I know that kind of friendship is very rare, but my friend Lauren and I have that same bond. I find that weird because I've known my best friend almost all of my life (since first grade) and it seemed that the characters also had known each other as long. Only a few people have the kind of special friendship that Lauren and I have. Your stories are about growing up and made me think about what middle school would be like.

I was reading about you and found out you do a lot of research before you write on one chosen topic. When you were writing about a deaf person in a mystery you actually went to schools for the deaf. I think that shows you really care about what you are writing. I also found that when you were going to write about a woman who lived in an Amish community, you stayed in an Amish community and helped out like you were one of them. While you were in the community you attended a wedding, helped around the garden, prepared dinner, and plucked, washed, cleaned, and cut the chickens so they were ready for dinner. All I have to say is *wow*! That is very unique and a very great thing because you really didn't have to do any of it . . .

Marly Kos

∽ ∽ ∽

Dear Marly,

What a terrific letter you wrote me! I really enjoyed it. You certainly did a lot of research, yourself. Where in the world did you get the information about my research on the deaf and on the Amish? I'm astonished, because neither of those books sold to publishers.

You obviously read a lot, Marly. (You're my kind of person.) I can tell that because you write very well.

I'll send you a favorite recipe; I'm trying to think of which one to choose. Because of a medical diagnosis seventeen years ago, I have to eat a low-fat diet, so my recipes won't please a lot of people.

You asked if I'm writing other books. Yes, I'm writing the third book in my "Dork" series. *Dork in Disguise* was the first. (It just won the Sequoyah Children's Book Award in Oklahoma! I'm very proud of that.) The sequel comes out at the end of May. It's called *Dork on the Run.* The third book—I'm a little over halfway finished—is called *A Midsummer Night's Dork.* It's supposed to be published in May 2003. [Now published.]

Thank you for your letter, Marly. I hope your class's recipe project goes well.

Best,
Carol Gorman

Recipe from Carol Gorman . . .

Chicken Soup with Wild Rice

Cooking Equipment:
Microwave dish
Cutting knife
Cutting board
Large saucepan
Measuring cup
Measuring spoons
Wooden spoon

Ingredients:
1 package boneless, skinless chicken breast
1 bunch green onions, sliced
1–2 tablespoons olive oil

5 carrots, peeled and diced
2 stalks celery, diced
8 ounces fresh mushrooms
2 tablespoons fresh parsley
2 quarts water
8 ounces wild rice
1 teaspoon sage
1 teaspoon thyme
1–2 tablespoons chicken-flavored Better Than Bouillon
$\frac{1}{2}$ cup white wine

Preparation:
1. Cook chicken breasts in microwave for 6–8 minutes. Set aside to cool.
2. Tear chicken breasts into small pieces and set aside.
3. Sauté green onions in oil and add carrots, celery, mushrooms, and parsley and cook until all vegetables are tender.
4. Add water, rice, herbs, and Better Than Bouillon.
5. Stir in chicken and simmer for 2 hours.
6. Add wine during the last twenty minutes of simmering.

SERVES 4–6

∾ ∾ ∾ ∾ ∾

Gail Carson Levine

Dear Gail Carson Levine,

I loved your novel *Ella Enchanted*! I was in fifth grade when I read it and I'm now in sixth. I think you're the best author ever! Your character detail is exquisite. I couldn't stop reading! Your book is full of adventure, cliffhangers, and emotions.

Is there going to be a sequel? I'd love to hear about it if there is. Your book has inspired me . . .

Kathleen McCarthy

∾ ∾ ∾

Dear Kathleen,

Thanks very much for your letter and I'm delighted that you enjoyed *Ella Enchanted*.

Here's a recipe for lettuce soup for your collection.

Thanks again for writing to me, and I hope the book is a great success!

Gail Carson Levine

Dear Gail Carson Levine,

I love your literature, especially *Ella Enchanted* because I greatly enjoy fantasies. I understand that through your writing you enjoy fairy tales. I have read and enjoyed all of your books. *Ella Enchanted* and *The Princess Tales* have inspired me to write like you. I greatly enjoy your work and I someday hope that I will be an illustrator for fantasies like yours.

I love to play soccer and in my free time I like to hang out with my friends, or even draw. I am Jewish too and it is interesting to hear about a Jewish author.

My family has had many recipes passed down through many generations. My father, being Italian, has had many Italian recipes passed down to him. My favorite is spaghetti with meatballs . . .

Julie Viola

∾ ∾ ∾

Dear Julie,

Thanks for your letter. I've already sent a recipe to one of your classmates, and I'm happy to be included in your project.

Best regards,
Gail Carson Levine

Recipe from Gail Carson Levine . . .

Lettuce Soup

Cooking Equipment:
    Cutting knife
    Cutting board
    Large pot
    Measuring cups
    Measuring spoons
    Wooden spoon
    Food processor
    Small mixing bowl
    Small saucepan

Ingredients:
    ¼ cup sliced scallions
    5 tablespoons vegetable oil
    1 head Romaine lettuce, shredded
    6 cups chicken broth
    1 teaspoon dried tarragon
    Pepper to taste
    1 teaspoon sugar
    1-pound package frozen peas
    2 tablespoons flour

Preparation:

1. In a large soup pot sauté scallions in 3 tablespoons of vegetable oil.
2. Add shredded lettuce and cook for 15 minutes over low heat until wilted.
3. Add chicken broth, tarragon, pepper, and sugar and cook for 20 minutes more.
4. Stir in ⅔ package of peas and bring to a boil.
5. Puree liquid mixture in a food processor, pour back into the soup pot, and return to low heat.
6. Mix together flour and remaining 2 tablespoons of oil.
7. Stir flour mixture into soup and cook until it is slightly thickened.
8. In a small saucepan, bring remaining peas to a boil and drain.
9. Serve soup and add peas as a garnish.

SERVES 4–6

൚ ൚ ൚ ൚ ൚

Jack Prelutsky

Dear Jack Prelutsky,

My name is Adam and I am a huge fan of yours! I enjoy reading novels, but I feel poetry allows you to stretch your imagination further. I adore your style of poetry and try to include it in some of the poems I've written. You are a big influence and I feel you are an excellent role model to young poets across the world.

I loved your poetry book called *A Pizza the Size of the Sun*. I have read all of your other poetry books and enjoyed each one very much. Some include *The New Kids on the Block* and *Something Big Has Been Here*. I have read each one over and over and still adore them to this day. As I read each poem, I was filled with mixed emotions. I got a good laugh out of each one but certain ones really caught my eye. You are an exquisite author and your poetry is superb.

A few years ago I dreamed of meeting you. Now I know I was pushing it a little, but I figured I should try writing to you . . . receiving your letter would be like a young boy receiving a Power Ranger toy for his birthday . . .

Adam Goldberg

൚ ൚ ൚

Dear Adam,

Thanks for sharing your poem with me. I enjoyed it, and hope you *keep writing*.

Cheers,
Jack Prelutsky

Recipe from Jack Prelutsky . . .

Looney Tuna

Cooking Equipment:
    Small mixing bowl
    Cutting knife
    Cutting board
    Measuring cup
    Measuring spoons

Ingredients:
    1 stalk celery
    1 stalk green onion
    1 apple
    1 can tuna, drained
    1–2 tablespoons mayonnaise—just enough to moisten
    ⅓ cup raisins
    A sprinkle of freshly grated black pepper

Preparations:
    1. Dice and chop vegetables and fruit.
    2. Mix all ingredients with tuna fish.
    3. Add mayonnaise, raisins, and black pepper.
    4. Serve on lettuce or toast.

    SERVES 2–4

℘ ℘ ℘ ℘ ℘

Dick King-Smith

Dear Dick King-Smith,

My name is Caroline and I am a very big fan of your writing. Overall, I like to read—not love—but when I picked up your book, *Babe: The Gallant Pig,* for school, I thought it was the best thing I had ever read. And just like that . . . I loved to read. Soon I had read every single one of your books, loving ALL of them. My favorite book was definitely *Martin's Mice.* I loved this because I have three cats, one being very much like Martin, her name is Annika. Her mom and dad are both fierce hunters, whereas she plays with the mice, and—believe it or not—takes naps with them. She is a very special kitty just like Martin.

I can not only relate to many of your books, but also admire them for one very special reason. From the author's notes in your stories, I have read that you were a farmer for twenty years. Taking that experience and putting that in your books makes it all the more special.

As I was researching you for this letter, I found out you prefer a typewriter, rather than new technology, to write your stories. Is there any particular reason why you do this? Do you have a computer or just a typewriter? Personally I think that using a typewriter is original, unique, and great. Your books are very special to me and I am a big fan . . .

Caroline Perry

∾ ∾ ∾

Dear Caroline,

I'm lucky enough to get thousands of fan letters from children all over the world, so many that I have to send them each a standard reply. But your letter was so special that I felt I would like to write you a proper letter.

I'm so pleased that *Babe* really turned you on to the joys of reading, and that you particularly liked *Martin's Mice*.

Incidentally, when I was farming, my favorite cat was actually called Dulcie Maude. She had 104 kittens in her lifetime.

I'm afraid I'm no good with machines, which is why I don't have a word processor or a computer or any of that sort of thing. I write in long hand in the mornings and type it out on this old portable in the afternoons. (I'm typing now because my handwriting is pretty awful and you probably couldn't read it.)

In due course I will send you some publishers' publicity stuff, which might interest you.

Now for that recipe. I think it a great idea that you donate any money you may make to the Children's Literacy Foundation.

Thanks again for your lovely letter.

Dick King-Smith

Recipe from Dick King-Smith . . .

Leek Onion and Potato Soup

Cooking Equipment:
   Cutting knife
   Cutting board
   Large saucepan
   Wooden spoon
   Measuring cups
   Measuring spoons
   Blender

Ingredients:
   4 large leeks
   4 tablespoons butter
   2 medium potatoes, peeled and sliced
   1 medium onion, chopped

Salt and freshly ground pepper
3 cups light chicken stock
1 cup milk
1½ tablespoons fresh, chopped chives
2 tablespoons cream

Preparation:
1. Trim off the tops and roots of the leeks, discarding the tough outer layer.
2. Spilt leeks lengthwise, slice finely, wash thoroughly, and drain well.
3. Melt butter in saucepan and add leeks, sliced potatoes, and onions and stir to coat with butter.
4. Season with salt and pepper, cover, and let vegetables sweat over a very low flame for 15 minutes.
5. Add stock and milk, bring to simmering point, and cover.
6. Simmer soup very gently for 20 minutes or until vegetables are soft.
7. Put mixture into a blender and puree.
8. Return soup to saucepan and reheat on a low flame.
9. Check seasoning by tasting soup, and then stir in chopped chives.
10. Add a swirl of cream just before serving.

SERVES 2–4

Author's Remarks:
The chilled version of this soup is called Vichyssoise.

Jane Yolen

Dear Jane Yolen,

I have only read a few of your books, and I can't wait to read more. I am a kind of fantasy person who is always searching for *dragons* because I wonder what I will learn next. When reading your novels it felt like I was in the book searching to destroy the wizards of the enchanted forests using lemon soup and water.

You have the talent to make older kids believe that they can still be filled with imagination, and that they don't have to fear it but can have fun with it.

The story that I am reading is *The Three of Solatia*. I haven't read that far yet, so I wonder if her daughter will find out about the king's seaweed jacket (that had three silver magic buttons), which he wore at his burial.

The other stories that I have read were *The Dragon's Blood* series. My friend loved it after I told her to read it. These stories are so inspiring that words cannot explain how it made me feel. It seems that I have trained the dragon and used my own saliva to heal his wounds. I always like to dream of what it would be like if I were the dragon trainer. It always gives me a happy feeling.

In many of your novels it seems as if you have had these adventures yourself. I mean, you write as if you came out of a dream, or what it could be like if more people believed in dreams and fantasies, instead of only *wishing* for them. Your stories truly come alive. . . . I am glad that you have such a writing talent . . .

Sara Allen

∾ ∾ ∾

Dear Sara,

Thank you for your letter about *The Pit Dragon Trilogy.*

I wrote *The Pit Dragon Trilogy* because I love dragons. Jakkin and Akki are based on my children who are now 30, 32, and 34 years old. In general, I get my ideas from the same place you get yours—from life.

In case you didn't pick up on the reference, Austar is named after Australia, which was a penal colony for the British two hundred years ago.

There are three books in *The Pit Dragon Series*: *Dragon's Blood, Heart's Blood,* and *A Sending of Dragons* and they are just being reissued by Magic Carpet/Harcourt Brace. I hope in the future to write a fourth book—if I can come up with a plot! But I have several other books with dragons in them: *Here There Be Dragon*s, *Merlin & the Dragons*, *Dove Isabeau,* and *The Dragon's Boy.*

In response to your request for a recipe of mine, I am including one of my favorites. Good luck with your project!

In case you want to know something more about me or my books, my new Web site address is: www.janeyolen.com.

Your book friend,
Jane Yolen

P.S. Thank you for your wonderful drawings too!
P.P.S. Your letter was one of the most literate I have ever gotten from a twelve to thirteen year old and a pleasure to read.

Recipe from Jane Yolen . . .

Carrot Soup à la Fiona

Cooking Equipment:
    Cutting knife
    Cutting board
    Measuring cups
    Large saucepan
    Blender
    Wooden spoon

Ingredients:
    2 tablespoons butter
    1 pound carrots, peeled, and sliced

1 onion, finely chopped
2 medium-sized potatoes, diced
Fresh coriander, if available
1–2 garlic cloves, peeled and minced
3 cups chicken stock
Freshly squeezed juice of 1 orange and its rind
Salt and pepper to taste
½ cup heavy cream

Preparation:

1. Melt butter in saucepan, add carrots, onion, potatoes, fresh coriander, and garlic and cook for 15 minutes on medium heat until tender.
2. Stir in chicken stock, orange juice, and rind.
3. Place in blender and puree.
4. Reheat soup by bringing to a low boil, add heavy cream, stir, and serve.

SERVES 2–4

ᘛ ᘛ ᘛ ᘛ ᘛ

5 ✌ Salads and Side Dishes

Morris Gleitzman

Dear Morris Gleitzman,

My name is Alice and I am a big fan of all your books. Overall, I like to read, but when I picked you your book *Blabbermouth,* it took me less than a day to read it. My favorite one though was *Gift of the Gab.* I loved the way you really gave me the feeling of how it would be like to be mute. It showed that just because they can't talk doesn't mean they're not smart or not able to participate like other kids.

It really touched me when they showed him playing the song her mother used to sing. I also enjoyed and was humored by the rotten apples incident. I was quite surprised as well when the supposed "poop" turned out to be her mother's favorite kind of meat.

While I read the book I was caught in a train of emotions, which I think makes you a very good author. At first I felt incredibly sorry for Rowena, but then I realized that even though she has a disability, her life is still pretty normal, I mean she lives in a house with her dad, like any other kid would. I was also able to feel and understand the seriousness for going to France.

I think you are a great author because you were able to put yourself in someone else's shoes without actually having that experience happen to you. Also you seem to have a moral in every book and I think that is very important for a child's book.

While researching you I noticed one of your favorite experiences in school was eating fries, is that still your favorite food? And that you prefer to write in a quiet place since you were seventeen. Now that you are older, do you have any other dream? If so, what is it? My dog likes your book too; just yesterday she was licking it . . .

Alice Rosenthal-Erickson

∾ ∾ ∾

Dear Alice,

Your letter seems to have taken ages to reach me here in Australia. Hope my recipe—which you have my permission to publish for charity—isn't too late. I'm glad you enjoyed *Gift of Gab*—Thanks for sharing your thoughts.

Best wishes,
Morris Gleitzman

Recipe from Morris Gleitzman . . .

Stir-Fried Spinach

Cooking Equipment:
Wok
Wooden spoon

Ingredients:

    3–4 tablespoons oil
    8–10 garlic chopped cloves
    2 sliced red chilies
    3–4 handfuls of English or Chinese spinach

Preparation:

    1. Heat oil in wok.
    2. Sauté chopped garlic and sliced red chilies for about 15 seconds.
    3. Add spinach.
    4. Stir-fry until wet and sloppy.

    SERVES 2

Author's Remarks:

    Add tofu if you need protein.

ɷ ɷ ɷ ɷ ɷ

Will Hobbs

Dear Will Hobbs,

    My name is Daniel. I read your book *The Maze.* I specifically liked this novel because part of it has to do with nature and saving the animals. I like to go hiking and biking on trails in the woods and that is why I like nature. I also read a lot of nonfiction books about endangered and not endangered animals.

    When I was reading your novel *The Maze,* I felt happy that someone was actually trying to save the California condor, which is endangered. I think you're the best author because all your books are about nature, are adventurous, and have action.

    What I think is very unique about you is that for your book, *Bearstone,* you wrote about a grizzly that really died, while they were supposed to be extinct in San Juan. Then when grizzles were spotted in San Juan, you wrote a sequel to *Bearstone* called *Beardance . . .* if you are on a new book, let me know in your letter back . . .

Daniel Ryan

ɷ ɷ ɷ

Hi Daniel,

    It was great to hear from you. I'm glad you're enjoying my books, most recently *The Maze*.

    Check at my Web site, www.WillHobbsAuthor.com, for an interview and photos for every book.

Enclosed is a great beans recipe that is an especially tasty treat for camping trips, potlucks, or while reading one of Will Hobbs' outdoor adventure tales! Very easy to prepare.

I am also enclosing a signed bookmark for you.

Will Hobbs

Recipe from Will Hobbs . . .

Yukon Beans

Cooking Equipment:
Heavy pan (cast-iron Dutch oven)
Cutting knife
Cutting board
Wooden spoon
Measuring spoon
Measuring cup

Ingredients:
½ pound bacon
2 small onions, sliced
1 large can of pork and beans
1 can of butter beans, drained
1 can of kidney beans, drained
½ cup brown sugar
¼ cup vinegar
¼ teaspoon dry mustard

Preparation:
1. Cut up bacon into small pieces and cook in heavy pan on medium heat.
2. Stir in sliced onions rings and sauté with the bacon.
3. Add pork and beans, butter beans, Kidney beans, brown sugar, vinegar, and dry mustard.
4. Simmer with lid on for 30 minutes, stirring occasionally.

SERVES 4

Author's Remarks:
This is good with barbecue and cole slaw.

∾ ∾ ∾ ∾ ∾

Brian Jacques

Dear Brian Jacques,

I have read many of your *Redwall* books including, *Mattimeo, The Long Patrol, Salamandastron, Martin the Warrior,* and *Pearls of Lutra.* These are some of the most interesting and fascinating books I have ever read in my life. I find these books so interesting because they have a lot of action and mystery. Your books contain so many new definitions of power and personalities of all the people around.

I love some exciting and good reading to make my day better, and your books are the kind that I read. You have such amazing books. They are some of my favorites because you add a series of medieval traditions, including animals.

My favorite two books of your series are *Mattimeo* and *The Long Patrol.* These include creative plots and villains. *Mattimeo* was especially good at the end in the recording from the *Redwall* recorder. You made the exciting story even more exciting in those last few pages, much unlike any other book that I've read.

The Long Patrol was also one of my favorite books because the way the Long Patrol and Redwall thought of a solution to their problem was very imaginative.

You are a truly great author with amazing ideas creating a world where mainly peace-loving creatures live . . .

Tim Ogino

ᘉ ᘉ ᘉ

Dear Tim,

Thank you for writing to me. I love to hear from young people like you who are so very enthusiastic about my work.

I enjoy my world of *Redwall* so very much, and I feel that over the years it has become more and more populated by characters I know and appreciate as friends. You and many others are there with me—peeping from behind pillars in the Abbey—looking down from the trees in *Mossflower* woods or waving to me from log boats on the River Moss.

My latest book is *Lord Brocktree,* a tale of a Badger Lord, and is now available in the U.K. and the U.S.A. My next *Redwall* book will be published in summer 2001 [now published], *Taggerung*—an otter warrior brought up by vermin, searching for his true home. Also, you can now join me in a new and exciting non-*Redwall* story, *Castaways of the Flying Dutchman.*

So as I journey again into my worlds I hope to see you there in Spirit. New villains and heroes are emerging and I am enjoying the adventure.

Keep reading and I will keep writing.

Sincerely,
Brian Jacques

Dear Brian Jacques,

Hi, my name is Alex. I am a sixth grader and a big fan of your work. Since I have read *Redwall,* I have read all the books in your series! They made me want to read more and more. There were many emotions I felt while reading them: happy, sad, excited, nervous, and I loved all the suspense. All the characters are cool. My favorite character in all of your books combined was Sunstripe, the badger. His bloodwrath was so cool and close behind him was Matthias, the mouse. You are the best author in my opinion. The books have so much detail. The wars are the good part. They are so realistically geared to the reader. I always think something is going to happen, and then you surprise me.

One unique fact I found out about you was that you started writing the *Redwall* books for children at a school for the blind. I think that will inspire new authors . . . also, when is your next book coming out? . . .

Alex Rosenberg

Dear Brian Jacques,

Hi. I have read the entire *Redwall* books, from *Redwall* to *Lord Brocktree.* I think that all of them are *awesome!!!* I love to read. Reading is one of my hobbies and I like to read a lot. This particular series was one of the best I've ever read. I love the style that you use to describe the characters, such as Gonff from *Mossflower* and Cluny from *Redwall.* I also love the way you incorporate humor in your stories. For example, I think the way you make the hares sound British is really funny. I also like the knowledge you have about the weapons in the story. They are just like medieval weapons.

I learned that you quit school at fifteen. Why didn't you continue school?

Overall, you utilize a lot of cliffhangers. You stop the most exciting parts to change the scene to a different place. I think this is really good writing because it makes the reader want to read on . . .

Chris Setian

ಎ ಎ ಎ

Dear Friends,

Thank you for writing to me.

It is wonderful to hear from readers who enjoy the food in my *Redwall* books. Many of my readers send me recipes that they or their families have developed based on the Redwall feasts, and which they have used at birthday parties.

I have chosen this family recipe for potato cakes (my family being half Irish) for you to include in your book.

This cookbook project sounds fun and delicious and I wish you every success!

Sincerely,
Brian Jacques

Recipe from Brian Jacques . . .

Potato Cakes

Cooking Equipment:
    Large saucepan
    Large mixing bowl
    Cutting knife
    Cutting board
    Potato masher
    Measuring cup
    Measuring spoons
    Flat surface for rolling and cutting
    Cookie sheet

Ingredients:
    1 pound of potatoes
    2 tablespoons butter
    ½ cup of grated cheese
    1 tablespoon chopped chives (or a little grated onion)
    ¼ teaspoon salt
    ⅛ teaspoon pepper
    1–2 level tablespoons of flour, if necessary

1 egg, beaten
¼ cup dry breadcrumbs

Preparation:
1. Preheat oven to 375°.
2. Peel, boil, and drain potatoes.
3. Mash potatoes in large bowl.
4. Mix mashed potatoes with butter, grated cheese, chives (or onion), and seasonings.
5. Beat until smooth, adding a little flour if necessary to make a firm mixture.
6. Turn onto a floured surface and form into a roll.
7. Cut into 1-inch slices and shape into round cakes.
8. Coat potato cakes with egg and dry breadcrumbs, place on a cookie sheet, and bake for 20 minutes.

SERVES 4–6

Author's Remarks:
Alternately, fry the cakes.

ॐ ॐ ॐ ॐ ॐ

Jerrie Oughton

Dear Jerrie Oughton,

I absolutely love your book, *Perfect Family*! I recently read it and greatly enjoyed it. I think you are a great author and what you write is literature at its best. I felt that *Perfect Family* really explained life, how someone or something could change so much over a small period of time, especially something as delicate and fragile as a family. Though I haven't experienced exactly what Welcome has, I feel that I can relate in a different sense.

Your book was one of the best I've ever read. Once I started reading it I couldn't put it down, I was completely drawn in. By the time I was done reading the story, it was as if I had been part of it all and personally knew all the characters; only the most talented of authors are able to do that . . .

Daniela Gil

ॐ ॐ ॐ

Dear Daniela,

Thank you for your lovely letter. The sun and stars and rainbow. (I need some stars and sun today because our cocker spaniel puppy ate my left house shoe last night. Of the black velvet pair with silver and gold suns and moons everywhere. My favorite pair, too. He was so proud of himself.) Thanks for the kind words about *Perfect Family*, also. It was an interesting book to write. I got so tired and sad from reading about young girls doing away with their unwanted infants that I wanted to do something to bring focus to that issue and perhaps show by example how a fictional character dealt with it.

A great many of the things that happened in the book really happened. The boy making the speech when he ran for student body president by standing on a thick book. Our daughters came home with that story. The boy and girl who were born in a Philippine concentration camp really lived "up" the street from us when I was growing up in Raleigh, NC. Their mom and my dad taught at the same college. I did not have a child out of wedlock, but I do remember the cutest girl in our 9th-grade class who suddenly quit coming to school. I know she got pregnant but not what happened to her.

What a delightful idea and I am happy to donate a recipe. When I wrote my first two books, picture books of two Navajo legends, someone told me I'd probably receive a lot of flak because I'm not Native American. So I developed an attitude. If a story is in my heart then I have the right to tell it. I guess that applies to recipes, also. I'm not Chinese either, but this recipe I'm sending is mighty good and you could say *it's in my heart,* too.

You might want to give the enclosed brochure to your teacher or librarian. I love to make school visits and do so all over the United States. In middle schools I talk to the students about the writing process, answer their questions, and tell the seeds of the novels. One in particular seems to make a lasting impression. Though the novel *Music from a Place Called Half Moon* tells the story of one summer in the life of a teenage girl in the mountains of North Carolina and a half-breed Indian boy, the story behind the book involves some Vietnamese boat people and how our family became friends with them when they moved to our small town and how I helped deliver their second baby.

Funding author visits can be a challenge but librarians find ways with book fairs and PTA funds. They cut corners by getting a nearby motel to donate a room or having the author stay in a student's home. When I was in high school our English teacher took us to visit a young novelist. I remember the evening to this day. He became a prolific writer and professor at Duke University—Reynolds Price. Among her students in those years were: Armistead Maupin and Anne Tyler. (If you haven't read Tyler's *Dinner at the Homesick Restaurant* you might find that fun.) Anyway, my point is that authors' visits carry quite an impact.

If your school can only afford someone nearby, my husband has a Web site on which he lists by region authors who love to visit schools. The address is: author-illustr-source.com.

Thanks again for the letter. Here's the recipe.

Sincerely,
Jerrie Oughton

Recipe from Jerrie Oughton . . .

Chinese Slaw

Cooking Equipment:
   Measuring cups
   Large bowl
   Wooden spoon

Ingredients:

1 cup sugar

1 cup olive oil (best if you use ¾ cup and add a little water)

⅔ cup white vinegar

2 packages of ramen noodles (with chicken flavor packets included)

1 cup slivered almonds (may be toasted at 305°). Not *silvered* as our kids used to laughingly call them.

½ cup sunflower seeds

1 16-ounce package shredded cabbage and carrots

6–8 chopped green onions (optional)

Preparation:

1. Combine sugar, olive oil, vinegar, and chicken flavoring from ramen noodle packages.
2. Add almonds and sunflower seeds to mixture.
3. Break up noodles and add to mixture, stirring well.
4. Stir in cabbage and carrots and toss to mix all ingredients.
5. Refrigerate overnight, stirring occasionally.

SERVES 10–12

Author's Remarks:

Makes a *lot*! And keeps several days because there's no mayonnaise involved. Enjoy!

∾ ∾ ∾ ∾ ∾

Diane Stanley

Dear Diane Stanley,

Your story *A Time Apart* really touched me because even though Ginny never wanted to go to England to visit her dad, she was now making the best of it, and she had made a new friend.

When my best friend moved away she told me the same thing that Ginny told Daisy. It brought back really good memories, and when I read that line about her writing letters, I stopped and sort of connected Ginny's life to mine, and it made me really happy, but I'm not quite sure why.

My name is Emily and until the beginning of this year, I wasn't much of a reader. When I read your book, I instantly fell in love with reading and now I read every day. But unfortunately no other book is as good as your *A Time Apart*. I love how you created Ginny's situation, going to visit her dad, and then including her in part of the Iron Age experiment.

While I was reading *A Time Apart,* I felt like I had known Ginny from when we were both really little. And each night I read, it was like I was reading a letter she was sending me from England to tell me about her trip. Your book is about a girl my age, and it is not totally an unbelievable book like some of them are, but aren't meant to be.

One thing I learned about you while researching was that you use your reading to create your writings. I find this very interesting because not many authors my friends are writing to said that they are very comforted by reading. I think this is a little strange because when I have to do a report for school I usually think back to the books I have read to make a connection between the two. And before I knew about you, I didn't know anybody else who did this too. I wonder if this is what told me to pick up your book or not, because it turned out to be my favorite book . . .

Emily Pape

ભ ભ ભ

Dear Emily,

Thank you for your lovely letter. After years of writing picture books, writing my first novel, *A Time Apart,* was very important to me. I put a lot of myself into the character of Ginny—and also of her parents, in different ways. Anyway, it pleases me to hear that the book touched you and seemed real. Maybe that was because I was writing from my heart. It is such a different kind of writing from the picture books and nonfiction I have done thus far. Things would just bubble up as I was writing that made me laugh or cry and I would think, *where did that come from?* Of course, it came from my own childhood, growing up not knowing my father, from losing my mother to cancer—so many things.

You strike me as a very thoughtful young lady. You write well and fluidly. It surprises me to learn that you have not been an avid reader all your life, because that is usually how young people get a grasp of language and learn to write well. I hope you will keep on finding joy and inspiration in books, now that you have started. If you have been disappointed by some you have tried, ask your librarian to suggest something you might like. I remember doing that as a kid and finding books I would never have read otherwise.

I am surprised to learn that the other authors who have written to your classmates have not mentioned a love of reading. I guarantee that they *do* love books, though. I have never met a writer who is not also a reader.

A recipe—hmmm. I do cook regularly for my family, but I am not a big user of recipes. I just kind of create as I go along. But I guess you need one, so here goes: Curried Chicken Salad.

Well, thanks again for your nice letter—and wonderful pictures, too. Good luck with your report and I hope you find many, many wonderful books to love. Have you read *Anne of Green Gables*? It was one of my favorites as a child.

All best wishes,
Diane Stanley

Recipe from Diane Stanley . . .

Curried Chicken Salad

Cooking Equipment:
    Frying pan
    Cutting knife
    Cutting board
    Bowl

Wooden spoon
Toaster oven or iron skillet

Ingredients:

2 boneless and skinless chicken breasts
Oil
Chicken broth
Scallions
Water chestnuts
Raisins (or apples or pears or dried cranberries—use your imagination)
Nuts (pecans, walnuts, almonds—whatever you like)
Curry powder
Mayonnaise
Salt and pepper
French bread

Preparation:

1. Cook the chicken breasts over low heat in a pan with a little oil and some chicken broth. Don't drown them, but you don't want them to dry out as they cook.
2. Let them cool sitting in the pan.
3. Pull the chicken apart into smallish pieces (I think this is nicer than cutting the meat into little squares) and put them in a bowl.
4. Dice the scallions (both white and green parts) and add them to the bowl. There is no specific amount—I happen to like a lot of onions in my chicken salad.
5. Drain the water chestnuts and cut them into little pieces. Again, no specific amount, but they will add a crunchiness, so you can decide for yourself how much you want. Add the raisins or other fruit to taste—again, I like a lot, especially if I'm using apples or pears. Dried fruit like raisins or dried cranberries tend to be stronger tasting, so use less.
6. Cut the nuts into medium to small pieces and toast them briefly in a toaster oven or in an iron skillet (no oil) over the burner. Just toast them a little so they crisp up. Add them to the bowl.
7. Add mayonnaise (or light mayonnaise, if you want to be healthy)—enough to bind all the ingredients into a salad.
8. Add a little curry powder, salt, and pepper to taste and mix it all together well.
9. Serve on toasted French bread.

SERVES 4–6

Author's Remarks:

Yum!

≈ ≈ ≈ ≈ ≈

6 ✅ Pasta and Sauces

Christopher Collier

Dear Christopher Collier,

My name is Clement. I am the kind of reader who requests a good book to read. The kinds of books I like to read are historical fiction and also nonfiction. I have read two of your books, which were *Jump Ship to Freedom* and *War Comes to Willie Freeman*. If you ask me, I think that your books were truly the finest I ever read, you truly write great literature. I especially liked the historical details that were in your book. The characters were great, especially Daniel, I really liked his personality. I also liked how every scene of your passages is described. If I close my eyes, I can see how Willie was in the long boat or how Daniel jumped off the *Junius Brutus*. On the Internet I also found out that you lived in a house built in 1790 with five fireplaces. It is great because you don't have to imagine what a house from the Revolutionary War period was like because you actually have one!

Our class is on a mission to help children learn to read and write . . .

Clement Bommier

∾ ∾ ∾

Dear Clement,

Thanks for your letter. I love getting all those wonderful words about our books.

I wish you well with your book. I do not cook very often, but when I do I make Glop.

I hope this helps.

Sincerely,
Christopher Collier

Recipe from Christopher Collier . . .

Glop

Cooking Equipment:
Large frying pan or skillet
Small bowl
Cutting knife
Cutting board
Measuring cups
Measuring spoons
Wooden spoon
Saucepan

Ingredients:

$\frac{1}{2}$ pound of hamburger meat

2 red peppers

2 green peppers

$\frac{1}{4}$ cup chopped onions

$\frac{1}{4}$ cup chopped mushrooms

4-ounce jar of pimientos

1–2 tablespoons of oil

Salt, pepper, and oregano to taste

12–16 ounces of tomato sauce

1 cup of rice or more

Preparation:

1. In a large frying pan, cook hamburger meat, drain grease, and set meat aside in a small bowl.
2. Fry chopped peppers, onions, mushrooms, and pimientos in hot oil until tender.
3. Season with salt, pepper, and oregano. (I add oregano liberally.)
4. Add tomato sauce to fried vegetables and simmer for 20 minutes.
5. Add cooked hamburger meat to tomato mixture, stir, and heat thoroughly.
7. Cook rice in separate saucepan.

SERVES 6–8

Author's Remarks:

You now have a nice hearty sauce to pour liberally over the rice. Serve with a green salad.

Irene Dunlap

Dear Irene Dunlap,

My name is Kate. I'm 12 years old and I'm in sixth grade. In my family, I have a mom, a dad, a sister, a cat (named Fluffy and is a male), and a fish (named Mr. Fish, but we have yet to know what gender!) My cat is 3 years old and is turning 4 on June 1st. Do you have any animals at home? I found out that you traveled around the world with the Semester at Sea for college. That is so cool! What was it like? I also know that you are an active member of a church's music team. Which church?

I have read many books in my life, but none have touched me more than your *Chicken Soup for the Pre-teen Soul*. The story that touched me the most was the story "Everything Will Be Okay." I think that it's wonderful that you put together stories like these to help kids with problems, or to make them feel better about what is happening to them or their family. It's also a terrific book to read for fun! I love to read books that are fairly big. That way I can enjoy it for many days. I also like to read books that are funny, about animals, action-packed, page-turning, and ones that are very hard to put down.

In my reading class, my classmates and I are trying to put together a children's book . . . I truly think that your book is the greatest and I think you are too . . .

Kate Sullivan

ᔆ ᔆ ᔆ

Dear Kate,

Thanks so much for your letter last June. I'm sorry it has taken a year to respond! We get *sooo* much mail it's nuts! How are Fluffy and Mr. Fish? I hope everything is going great for you and that you had a good school year. I have no idea if you are still making that book, but just in case, I'm enclosing my favorite recipe for clam linguini. It has fresh steamers in it!

Thanks for the wonderful compliment of being asked to participate in your book. I wish you the best and hope that you will achieve your highest goals.

Blessings,
Irene Dunlap

Recipe from Irene Dunlap . . .

Irene's Secret Clam Linguini Sauce

Cooking Equipment:
Large saucepan for sauce
Large pot for linguini
Wooden spoon
Chopping knife
Cutting board
Measuring cups
Measuring spoons

Ingredients:
1½ tablespoons butter
3–4 tablespoons chopped shallots or white onion
4–6 chopped medium garlic cloves
2 teaspoons tarragon
1 teaspoon basil
½ teaspoon oregano
½ teaspoon fine herbs (see Glossary)
Pepper to taste (no salt)
1 can chopped clams with juice
Additional 4 ounces of clam juice
½ cup dry white wine
Littleneck or cherrystone clams (4–6 per person)
½–1 cup of fresh cream (depending on desired thickness)
¾ cup chopped tomatoes
4–5 chopped green onions

Package of linguini
Freshly grated Parmesan cheese

Preparation:
1. Sauté chopped shallots in butter over low heat.
2. Add chopped garlic cloves and stir.
3. Add tarragon, basil, oregano, fine herbs, and pepper to taste.
4. Add chopped clams with juice, 4 ounces of additional clam juice, and dry white wine.
5. Add littleneck or cherrystone clams and stand them up in pan so they steam open.
6. Cover and simmer until stock reduces to ½–¾ cup.
7. Remove clams if cooked and steamed open, then set aside.
8. Add fresh cream and stir well.
9. Add chopped tomatoes and green onions and stir.
10. Pour sauce over al dente linguini. (Cook linguini as you are preparing the sauce.) Top with steamed clams and freshly grated Parmesan cheese.

SERVES 4–6

ஒ ஒ ஒ ஒ ஒ

Claudine Gandolfi

Dear Claudine Gandolfi,

In your book *Sisters,* I very much agree with you, why, what can be said from the bond of sisterhood. It does cause closeness and beyond any compare. I have a sister and we share rooms, and

I borrow her clothes all the time! We fight a lot, but we always make up a day later. I loved your thoughts on sisters, I mean it's all true and I compare myself to the book when I read it. No one could understand you like your own sister. I liked that you also put in other peoples thoughts on sisters. It broadens the idea of what the book is all about. I like your idea about sisters being your conscience and also how they can also be your confidence because my sister and I share that all the time.

I like you as my favorite author because you really took a part of life, to make everyone know how important having a sister is. You said the truth; thoughts of sisterhood are expectable for all people to know. I hear you have a sister named Michele, you said she was your sister, your friend, and your shadow. I really admire that. I think from reading this book it made me feel like I was bonding more with my sister. Realizing how important she is, we haven't had a fight in 5 months.

Do you have a brother? I have one, his name is William, and we like to call him Liam for short. He is six years old, and a lot of fun to be with. We also have a bond. Did you ever write a book on brothers, or mothers and their daughters? If you did I would love to read them! I know that you've written *World's Best Mom, Little Christmas Treasures, Night Before Dog-Mas,* and *Catmas, Best Friends, A Sister Is a Best Friend, Teachers Make a Difference,* and many more. I've only read so far *Sisters,* but I love what you write, and I'm going to try to read the rest. It would be nice to hear from you . . .

Alexa Derkasch

∾ ∾ ∾

Dear Alexa,

The publisher passed your letter on to me.

Thank you so much for taking the time to let me know that you enjoyed the *Sisters* book that I wrote. It really means a lot to me to know what you thought of the book. I'm glad you and your sister are getting along better now. You may find this interesting: My sister Michele wrote a sequel, *Sisters Always.*

I haven't written anything on brothers, simply because I don't have one. I'm sure there are other writers out there who could do the topic justice from having experienced that connection in real life. On mothers I've written a few titles, some of which you listed in your letter.

As for my favorite recipe, it's tough. I'd have to say that it would have to be my grandmother's pasta sauce. Her mother taught her how to make it and she passed it along to my sister and me. She used it on everything from pasta, to ravioli (which we all still make together on Christmas Eve), to rice. The most important ingredient is the porcini mushroom, which, luckily for my family, grow wild in the part of Italy that my family originally came from. They're expensive to buy in stores.

I think your class is doing a great thing by putting together this recipe book for the Children's Literacy Foundation. Please let me know how successful it is.

I've also enclosed my little book on Celtic (Irish, Scottish, etc.) legends that you may enjoy, plus a cool little gift book set on self-esteem for young teens. I hope you enjoy them. Best of luck to you!

Sincerely,
Claudine Gandolfi

Recipe from Claudine Gandolfi . . .

Great-Grandma Toma's Porcini-Meat Sauce

Cooking Equipment:
2 large frying pans
Measuring spoons
Cutting knife
Cutting board
Large pot
Small saucepan
Measuring cup
Wooden spoon

Ingredients:
2 tablespoons oil
3–4 stalks celery chopped
3 medium onions chopped
2 pounds of ground veal/pork/beef blend
¾ cup dry porcini mushrooms
2 cups water
1 clove garlic chopped
1 28-ounce can Italian crushed tomatoes
Salt and pepper to taste
1 cube beef bouillon plus 1 cup water (if necessary)

Preparation:
1. Heat oil over medium heat, add chopped celery and onions, and sauté until tender.
2. Fry meat blend in separate pan, drain, and add to vegetables.
3. Wash porcini mushrooms in warm water and drain.
4. Cook mushrooms in small saucepan with 2 cups of water for 30 minutes.
5. Add garlic, mushrooms, and water to meat/onion blend.
6. Pour in can of crushed tomatoes and stir.
7. Add salt and pepper to taste.
8. Reduce sauce by simmering for approximately 3 hours.
9. If sauce becomes too thick, add one dissolved beef bouillon cube in water to thin out mixture.

SERVES 4–6

❧ ❧ ❧ ❧ ❧

E. L. Konigsburg

Dear E. L. Konigsburg,

My name is Victoria. I am a sixth grader and attend middle school. You are my all-time favorite author and I've read about ten of your books. I particularly liked *The View from Saturday, From the Mixed-Up Files of Mrs. Basil E. Frankweiler,* and *T-backs, T-Shirts, Coat, and Suit.*

I wrote this letter as part of a project to spread the word of reading. My teacher hopes that if kids around the country can take a look at the book, they will read the author's line and be inclined to read the book that is mentioned on the page, or they may even go as far as doing the recipe. The child would probably tell one of their friends about a good book, and from there, the word of reading would be spread.

I personally would never cherish life as much as I do now without the joy of reading. There are many books that I find are good to read for plot, suspense, and characters, and that's why I like your book *From the Mixed-Up Files of Mrs. Basil E. Frankweiler.* Moreover, there is much to learn from reading, especially books that have a good theme, such as two of your books: *The View from Saturday* and *T-backs, T-Shirts, Coat, and Suit.* They show, respectively, that kindness and caring can mean much and that it is okay to be yourself when the world seems to be divided or leaves you out. That is why I like those books: because of theme (often that is a reason that I like most books), so I chose to write to you instead of another author. Right now, I am looking for another of your books to read, since I have already read ten I could find in the library . . .

Victoria Tan

∾ ∾ ∾

Dear Victoria,

In recent years I have developed a bad attitude toward the kitchen, but before that, I loved this recipe. I still sometimes make it on special occasions.

Best wishes for the success of your project.

E. L. Konigsburg

Recipe from E. L. Konigsburg . . .

Betty Ellovich's Mother-in-Law's Lokchen Kugel

Cooking Equipment:
Saucepan
13½ × 8¾-inch Pyrex dish
Eggbeater
Measuring cups
Measuring spoons
Wooden spoon

Ingredients:
- 1 stick of butter ($\frac{1}{4}$ pound)
- 8 ounces medium noodles
- 3 eggs, beaten
- 3 tablespoons sugar
- 1-pound container creamed cottage cheese
- 1 cup sour cream
- 1 can crushed pineapple, drained

Topping:
- 4 handfuls of crushed cornflakes
- 3 handfuls of brown sugar

Preparation:
1. Preheat oven to 350°.
2. Boil noodles and drain.
3. Melt butter and place in Pyrex dish.
4. Mix all of the above ingredients with boiled noodles.
5. Pour mixture in buttered baking dish.
6. Top with 4 handfuls of crushed cornflakes and 3 handfuls of brown sugar.
7. Bake for 1 hour.

SERVES 8

Note:
This recipe may be used as a side dish as well.

Elvira Woodruff

Dear Elvira Woodruff,

I read your book the *Orphan of Ellis Island* and thought it was so great that I read it two more times! My name is Nicole and I am in the sixth grade. One of your books that I have read most recently is *The Magnificent Mummy Maker*. I liked this book a lot because it was so mysterious and it always left me on a cliffhanger. Books like that are always the ones I like the best. But my favorite out of all your books is *Orphan of Ellis Island*. I felt this way because I liked how you had Dominic solve his problem by time traveling. I liked this because it is not the way problems are usually solved. I also liked how Dominic got to learn about his ancestors but in a mysterious way. While I was reading your book I felt very anxious to find out what would happen next. I was saddened when Salvador died on their way to the ship, but I became happy again when Dominic safely returned from the past. I also like how you can take a problem that could happen and turn it into such a realistic problem. I found some things about you that were really unique like how you were born in Raritan, NJ, a town not far from where I live! I also can't believe your first job was as a janitor at an office building. What gave you the idea to do that? You are unique to me in one other way and that is how you change jobs so many times before knowing what you should be in your life. It is interesting how you didn't even know you were going to be an author and now you are an extremely famous writer! I have a few questions to ask you, the first one is: Out of all the jobs you experienced before becoming a writer, which one did you like best? My other question is: Do you think you will ever stop wanting to write? I hope you don't because I love reading your books . . .

Nicole Longo

P.S. My reading teacher reads us poems from a poetry book called *Sawgrass Poems,* which your cousin, Frank Asch, wrote. Every spring we read these poems when we study a unit called *Our Living Earth.* Enclosed is a letter written by a student named Heidi, who wrote to your cousin but he didn't respond. If you don't mind could you give this to him the next time you see him, for her?

∾ ∾ ∾

Dear Nicole,

Thanks for your letter. I get so much mail from readers I'm afraid I have to print up one letter for everyone, but I have included a special P.S. just for you! I'm living in Martins Creek, Pennsylvania, which is very close to the Delaware River. Often times an author is inspired by her neighborhood. My book *George Washington's Socks* is set along the Delaware during the Revolutionary War. So poke around your neighborhood and see if there isn't some great story there for you to tell.

People, family, and friends can often inspire a story. My own two sons, Noah and Jess, inspired my book *Awfully Short for the Fourth Grade.* My Uncle Crescenzo inspired *Dear Napoleon I Know You're Dead* and my grandparents were the inspiration for my *Orphan of Ellis Island.*

So keep your ears and eyes open around the house. Try jotting down the goofy things your little brother does at the dinner table, or the funny way your father yawns, the way your mother sings out of tune when she's driving to the store, or the way your dog likes to eat the dust balls under your bed. And before you know it you'll have all the interesting characters you'll need for a story.

My new book out last year was *The Christmas Doll.* This is the story of two orphaned sisters, living in London in the 1800s. The girls find a very special doll they call Morning Glory. If you like dolls, morning glories, and Christmas you might give this one a try.

Readers always want to know what new book I'm working on. After a visit to the Tower of London I decided to write a book about a boy who helps a girl escape from the Tower. So, if you'd like to read about a very brave boy living in a very interesting place and the spirited girl he manages to rescue, stay tuned!

P.S. Nicole, I was glad to hear that you liked my *Orphan of Ellis Island.* I had a great time dreaming that one up. To answer your questions—the job I loved most besides writing was working as a gardener. If you ever get a chance to work for a rich person on their estate as a gardener, don't pass it up. They have beautiful gardens and because they are so rich they have many houses and so are hardly ever home. That means that you get to work in a beautiful garden day after day, while your boss is off to some far-flung place. To answer your second question—I honestly don't know if I'll ever stop wanting to write—maybe—but that's ok. Writing is wonderful, but so is baking a pie or painting a picture or going for a walk in the woods. I can think of lots of things I like doing and if

I do stop writing I'll just do them! I am enclosing a recipe (one of the other things I love doing is cooking). And I sent your letter to my cousin, Frank. He does go to Florida every winter to escape the Vermont cold so that might be why you haven't heard from him. Have a most creative year, Nicole, and May the Muse Be with You . . .

Best,
Elvira Woodruff

Recipe from Elvira Woodruff . . .

Penne Perfecto

Cooking Equipment:
Cutting knife
Cutting board
Measuring cups
Measuring spoons
13×9×2-inch baking dish (glass or lasagna tray)
Small bowl
Large frying pan or skillet
Medium frying pan
Wooden spoon
Large pot

Ingredients:
6 peppers cut into strips (3 green and 3 red or any assortment you choose)
6 tablespoons olive oil
Salt and pepper
2 garlic cloves coarsely cut
½–1 cup finely chopped fresh or dry parsley
1 tablespoon finely chopped fresh or dry oregano
1 tablespoon fresh or dry thyme
1 pound sliced white mushrooms
1 pound sweet Italian sausage (squeeze it out of the casing and cut into little bits as you fry it)
1 pound Penne pasta
¼ cup reserved pasta cooking liquid (or just water if you forget to save it)
Grated Parmesan cheese to taste

Preparation:
1. Preheat oven to 450°.
2. Place cut peppers in baking dish, drizzle 3 tablespoons of olive oil on top, and add salt and pepper.
3. Bake peppers 30–40 minutes or until tender and charred on edges; stir occasionally.
4. Remove peppers from oven when tender and set aside.
5. Combine chopped garlic and chopped herbs in a small bowl and set aside.

6. Heat remaining 3 tablespoons of oil in a frying pan, add sliced mushrooms, and sauté until tender and golden brown.
7. Add garlic and herb mixture and sauté for 2 minutes more.
8. Sprinkle with salt and pepper to taste, then add baked peppers.
9. Place sausages in a separate frying pan over medium heat and cook until brown, then drain.
10. Add cooked sausages to the pepper mixture, cover, and keep in warm oven.
11. Cook penne by package directions, approximately 12 minutes, and save ¼ cup of the pasta water.
12. Add pasta and ¼ cup liquid to pepper, herb, and sausage mixture.
13. Stir it all up and sprinkle with Parmesan cheese.

SERVES 4–6

ؑ ؑ ؑ ؑ ؑ

7 ❧ Main Dishes

Joanna Campbell, a.k.a. Jo Ann Simon

Dear Joanna Campbell,

Hi! My name is Anne. I am writing to you because I love your books. I could probably take an educated guess that you love horses. Well, I think we are on the same page because I love them too! Your books are *so* great! You add so much detail that you make me feel like I am the one in the saddle. In my opinion, you are the best author that has ever written equestrian and equine novels.

My favorite part about your *Thoroughbred* series is when one of the horses is in a race, I feel like I am the one steering and controlling Pride, or Wonder, or Fleet Goddess. I have read all the books you have written up to number ten. My mom is getting me numbers eleven through fourteen soon and *I cannot wait* to start reading them. Again, whenever I read your novels you make the setting, mood, situations, and the conflicts so clear and perfect for the novel. You state the feelings of all the characters in such a way that you *are* the person feeling those feelings. Like for instance, the annoyed and sad feelings of Ashleigh, the flashbacks of Samantha's mother, and the greedy, prideful feelings of Brad Townsend.

The thing that I really love about every novel is the climax. They are always perfect, fitting right into the story. You paint such a great picture I actually thought the horses and the people in Townsend Acres and Whitebrook Farms were all real. I learned a lot about racing too! Like about the walking ring, the clubhouse turn, the marker poles on the track, and *a lot* more! You are probably thinking, "Gosh, she doesn't know a lot at all!" Well you are right. I do not know a lot now, but I am hoping to research a lot on racing. I want to become a jockey when I am older, like Jill and Ashleigh riding Pride like in your novel. I was looking on the Web for you and I could only find so much. I really tried . . .

P.S. If you get a chance, could you send me one of your all time favorite novels you wrote in the *Thoroughbred* series with your autograph? I would love that so much!!! It would mean *so much* to me. My favorite is . . . all of them . . .

Anne Molnar

∾ ∾ ∾

Dear Anne,

I would love to provide you more information about my background as a writer. I also have a Web site: www.joannacampbell.com.

I write under two names: Jo Ann Simon (adult books), and Joanna Campbell (young adult books). I've enjoyed writing for both genres, but the responses I receive from my younger writers truly warm my heart—especially when a reader writes me that she'd never liked reading until she started reading the *Thoroughbred* series. I think the major rational for writing a novel is to reach out to readers and in some way influence their lives positively. From the responses I've received over the last decade about the *Thoroughbred* series, I think I've accomplished that—and that connection means far more to me than any money I've received in writing the series, or any other of my books.

Writing always came naturally to me, and I've always had a vivid imagination. The first books I published (adult books) were romantic, time travel novels, where things that weren't supposed to happen did happen.

I've been a horse lover all my life, and it was my agent who got me started in writing for the young adult audience about horses. In writing all of my horse books, I've drawn on my own dreams and frustrations while growing up, when I tried to convince my parents to take my love of horses seriously and get me a pony. My grandfather had fields and a barn next door, where he offered to stable my pony or horse.

But my parents believed my interest was temporary—that my interests would change, as I got older—and that they would end up being responsible for my horse.

My interests did change somewhat when I got into my teens, and stopped thinking of boys as adversaries, but as dates. Yet my love for horses never died.

I finally got, until then, my lifelong wish of owning a horse in my early twenties, married mother of an infant daughter, when friends took us to a sale of horses bought up from abusive stables.

Although I'd ingested horse lore and read every horse book written from the time I was ten, I'd never actually learned how to ride, since I had no free access to horses. None of the horses in that field looked well cared for. Some were bigger and healthier than others, but because of my lack of confidence as a rider, I chose one of the smaller ones—just under fifteen hands—to ride. All the horses and their ragged winter coats, but the chestnut horse I chose to ride plodded under me rather than running off with an inexperienced rider.

My husband and I bought him for one hundred dollars. We boarded him free at a friend's place before bringing him to a makeshift but adequate paddock at my parents, which my father helped me build. He'd put on some weight at our friends by getting fed regularly, but he was still skin and bones and listless, and I found out why that spring when I brushed away his winter coat—he was crawling with lice.

After talking to our last livestock provisioner in town, I found out what to use to get rid of the lice, and sprayed and combed Moe accordingly. To make a long story short, Moe filled out, prospered, and his chestnut coat shined. A cousin helped me to teach him to jump, and he showed us what a natural cutting horse he has been in an earlier part of his life by trying to round us up in an open field when no one was in his saddle.

That's my story with Moe.

I later went on to take serious lessons, when I could afford to pay for them myself, and learned the highs and lows of open jumping. When it was good, it was superb; when it was bad, it was devastating, i.e., broken bones and a hit on your confidence.

Much of those experiences have been relayed into the *Thoroughbred* series, although I wrote about horse racing, not jumping (I have books outside the series about jumping).

But the connection between rider and horse is the same, whether it be racing, jumping, or Western reining. To succeed, you have to be a pair. You have to know your horse, and your horse has to know you.

One of my favorite things is taking a horse out of its stall, putting it in crossties, and grooming and talking to the horse at the same time. I love to find the spots in grooming that help the horse relax. I love to find the point when the horse and I have a meeting of the minds—horses do have thinking minds, and you can talk to them if you realize that their impulses for survival are very different from your own.

P.S. Since writing this letter, my granddaughters and I have purchased a quarter horse named Horizon. He just turned five. He's a chestnut with a wide white blaze. We love him.

Okay, that covers a lot of what I haven't said about myself. Now my recipe for eggplant parmesan.

Hope this helps you, Anne. I'll also be sending along an autographed book. And if you have any further questions for me, please e-mail me and ask them. And tell your classmates and friends that they can do the same.

My best to you and your school! May the Horse be with You!

Joanna Campbell

P.S. In the signed book I've sent, my message to you may seem big and sloppy, but it is very hard to write clearly in the confines of a book jacket.
P.P.S. And *I loved* your drawings!

Recipe from Joanna Campbell . . .

Eggplant Parmesan

Cooking Equipment:
Cutting knife
Cutting board
Measuring spoons
Large frying pan
2 mixing bowls
6×12-inch baking pan

Ingredients:
1 good-sized eggplant
1 or 2 eggs, beaten
Several tablespoons of milk
1 cup seasonal Italian breadcrumbs
Olive oil as needed for frying
Parmesan, Romano, and mozzarella cheeses, all grated
1 jar (2–3 cups) of marinara sauce
1 packet of Italian sweet sausages, optional

Preparation:
1. Preheat oven to 350°.
2. Cut eggplant into thin slices.
3. Combine egg and milk, drench eggplant slices in mixture, and coat both sides with breadcrumbs.
4. Fry eggplant slices in hot olive oil, adding more olive oil as needed until eggplant is browned on both sides.
5. If using sausages, split sausages in half, lay them uncooked over the bottom of baking dish, and place a layer of eggplant slices on top. For vegetarians, make the bottom layer of your baking dish crispy, browned eggplant slices.
6. Cover lightly with a good Italian tomato sauce and a layer of grated Italian cheeses—a mixture of Parmesan, Romano, and perhaps mozzarella.

7. Repeat with a layer of eggplant slices, a topping of tomato sauce, and grated cheeses.
8. Repeat step 7 until all eggplant slices are used.
9. Bake for 30–40 minutes.

SERVES 4

Author's Remarks:

Not all the eggplant slices will fit into frying pan: This procedure will have to be repeated about four times. Also, sauce may be homemade or store-bought. I prefer Classico store-bought sauce—any variety will do, but I generally use their garlic/sundried tomato mix. I would also suggest tasting the prepared sauce to see if your own taste buds find anything lacking—like garlic, or the spiciness of oregano, or the saltiness. If you find any deficiencies, add (sparingly) more of the ingredients you feel the sauce is lacking.

Voilà, a feast!

Robert Davies

Dear Robert Davies,

Hello, my name is Christine and I am in middle school. In my school for reading class we picked our favorite authors to write to and I chose you. When I read how the simplest times in life can make you the happiest, I knew I wanted to read *Mayhem on Maui* because I like the opening paragraph in the form of a question. I think it makes it kind of interesting for the reader. I liked the character KC because you formed her character so well and you give *so* much detail. You have a great vocabulary and a wide spread of words; I even had to look some of them up. You use a lot of suspense by setting up coincidences in the story. At that point it makes you want to read on because you don't know how the characters knew each other. You also use cliffhangers that also make you want to read on! I felt many things in this book because it went from miserable to cheerful all in the same chapter. I think you're the best author because when I read your book I was so amazed at how well you wrote the book! I haven't been able to find a book lately I could really enjoy and then when I got your book for Christmas I started reading it. Thank you so much for calling me back, it meant the whole world to me! Thank you for the biographical information too . . .

Christine Henderson

Dear Christine,

Thank you so much for your lovely letter. You seem to be a very dynamic young lady, and I encourage you to stay on that track, as it will give you a very interesting life. Let me try and answer your questions.

First of all, there is a new KC book in the works called *Rampage on the Riviera*. [Now published.] As a scoop, I enclose a little excerpt at the end of this e-mail.

Secondly, I would be very happy to offer a recipe for your project with Mrs. Waltz. Instead of mailing it to your teacher I am enclosing it here so you can print it out and give it to her.

The recipe is for seafood fritters, and it is really yummy. You can replace the given contents with just about anything you like, by the way.

Best of luck,
Robert Davies

Recipe from Robert Davies . . .

Seafood Fritters

Cooking Equipment:
    2 large mixing bowls
    Wooden spoon
    Slotted metal spoon
    Large frying pan
    Paper towels

Ingredients:
    2 pounds or a little more mixed raw seafood:
    Diced shrimp, minced cod, haddock, or other white-fleshed fish
    Crab meat (frozen—unfreeze before using—or canned)
    Mussels (meat of freshly cooked mussels), optional
    Lobster or crawfish.
    1 teaspoon mild or hot paprika, according to your taste
    Pinch of salt
    1 cup flour and slightly more
    ½ teaspoon salt
    3 eggs (1 whole and two whites only, kept separate)
    1 tablespoon oil
    ¼–½ cup beer or water
    Enough oil to deep fry

Preparation:
    1. Mix the seafood together with the paprika and a pinch of salt and set aside (the mixture can stand at room temperature for an hour, but if you are cooking after a longer delay than that, keep the mixture in the fridge until you are ready to fry). If using mussels, discard the shells after you steam them or cook them in just an inch or two of water for 5 minutes.
    2. Mix the flour, salt, the whole egg, and the oil with a wooden spoon.
    3. Slowly add the beer, or water if you must, to obtain a thick batter, which must be left at least 1 hour in the fridge to set.

4. When the batter has sat for at least an hour in the fridge, beat the 2 egg whites into a thick froth and fold them into the batter (they will make it light as a feather!).
5. Combine the batter with the seafood mixture.
6. Heat your oil in a deep fryer, and when it is good and hot but not smoking, form your fritters with a large tablespoon and cook as many fritters as your fryer can handle at once, while keeping the oil properly hot. (Nothing is worse than soggy fritters cooked at lower than best heat!)
7. When the fritters are nicely crisp on the outside, medium brown but not burned, drain on paper towels and pop them in your mouth. Or put them in the oven on low heat if you are gathering them to put on the table all at once.

SERVES 4–6

Author's Remarks:

When they are all ready, serv 'em up hot and delicious! Ketchup is *not* required, but lemon slices are good, and Tabasco sauce doesn't hurt either. If you feel fancy, a bit of mayonnaise mixed with crushed garlic will also do just fine. The beauty of this recipe is you can throw in whatever you like, even some corn niblets or diced red pepper or little bits of cooked bacon.

Kate DiCamillo

Dear Kate DiCamillo,

Hi, my name is Tara. I am a huge fan of your work. Your book *Because of Winn-Dixie* really hooked me. I love the theme. I liked how you had a girl who wanted a dog so bad, yet she did not just get it. She had to work and earn it. Reading your book opened up a whole new way of reading to me. It was fun! When I read your book, I noticed there were a lot of different emotions and moods, for example: When Opal brought back the dog, she was very happy; when her Dad said, "I'll think about it," she was extremely anxious, along with many other emotions. I thought it was really neat how you tied them all together. I think you are a fantastic writer. I like how you used details. This helps the reader make a picture in their mind. When I grow up I want to be an author just like you. The other night I was doing some research on you so I could write this letter. I learned that you wrote this book partially because you missed your dog. Another detail I found out about you made me extremely excited because after I read it I knew you would write back to me! This detail I found out was that your favorite award was when a kid wrote you a letter saying, "I liked your book, and will you write me another one" and you did . . .

Tara Maxwell

Hey Tara,

Thanks for your great letter. I'm glad you loved *Because of Winn-Dixie*. Sad to say, I don't cook *at all,* so I can't send you a recipe for your book. But I do send you my affection, my warm wishes and my hope that you will keep reading and writing.

All best,
Kate DiCamillo

Tara, Okay!

I talked to my mom and here is her recipe for one of my favorite dishes: Chili con Carne.

Kate DiCamillo

Recipe from Kate DiCamillo . . .

Chili con Carne

Cooking Equipment:
Cutting knife
Cutting board
Large frying pan

Ingredients:
¼ cup chopped onions
1 pound hamburger meat
2 cans of dark red kidney beans
2 cans of Campbell's tomato soup
Dash of chili powder, optional

Preparation:
1. Chop onions and put in frying pan with hamburger meat.
2. Brown meat and onions.
3. Add dark red kidney beans and tomato soup.
4. Add chili powder to taste.
5. Let simmer for at least 1 hour; stir occasionally.

SERVES 4–6

Author's Remarks:
Yum.

৩ ৩ ৩ ৩ ৩

Martha Freeman

Dear Martha Freeman,

Hi, my name is Mary and I am a great fan of yours. I'm writing to you because when I read the book, *The Year My Parents Ruined My Life,* I fell in love with it! When I read the first line of the book it struck me because it's my friend's name almost exactly. I've also had the recent experience of several friends moving and I could relate to the story. Your cliffhangers were great, such as when Kate was in the process of running away, also known as "Operation Defrost," they made me more excited and anxious to read the book and see what would happen next. Also the way you described how Kate hated Belletoona so much, I could understand why she disliked it. I felt scared when I didn't know what was going to happen, for example when Kate was caught with drugs, and you didn't know what was going to happen. I felt happy too, when Kate didn't mind living there (in Belletoona) and she had found out that Belletoona wasn't so bad all of the time and suspense when you left a cliffhanger. You are such a great author for your great descriptions, your cliffhangers, and humor, when I (the reader) wanted to have some fun. I thought Kate was a very humorous character at times. You always made the character do the right thing too, most of the time . . .

Mary Morano

∾ ∾ ∾

Dear Mary,

Thanks for your very long letter about *The Year My Parents Ruined My Life*. I am glad you enjoyed it so thoroughly and read it so carefully.

It is fun for me to see that kids all over the country like that book.

You didn't ask me any questions about the book (most kids do!), but I am going to tell you a little about it anyway. Otherwise I don't think it will be much like a Christmas when you and your class open this letter.

When I was twelve my family spent the summer on Balboa Island, which is south of Los Angeles. Isla Nada is based a lot on my memories of Balboa.

I changed schools twice as a child, but what's more important to the book is that my family moved from Sonora, California, to State College, Pennsylvania, in 1995. Two towns near State College are Altoona and Bellefonte—so I put those two names together and came up with Belletoona. When I wrote the book, I was thinking about my oldest daughter Sylvie, who didn't want to move. She was eight at the time. I have two other children, Rosa and Ethan. We have two cats, a dog, and a fish named Louis.

I didn't really write the book with the idea of delivering a message to kids, but I have noticed that most often in life things do work out—not always the way you expect them to. And that's what happens to Kate.

As it happens, I like to cook and to exchange recipes. I just happen to have this all typed and ready to go. I am not a—very—strict vegetarian as are my two daughters. My husband and son eat vegetarian at home because they don't have a lot of choice. This recipe enables us to enjoy "hamburgers" without any meat.

I also enclosed some bookmarks for you, your friends, and Mrs. Waltz. Yes, I think your cookbook is a great idea, and I hope it raises lots of money for a good cause.

Keep reading!

Sincerely,
Martha Freeman

Recipe from Martha Freeman . . .

Chili Burgers

Cooking Equipment:
  Cutting knife
  Cutting board
  Frying pan
  Measuring cups
  Measuring spoons
  Large mixing bowl
  Potato masher
  Frying pan
  Nonstick skillet

Ingredients:
  1 cup chopped onions
  4 minced garlic cloves
  1–2 tablespoons olive oil for sautéing
  $\frac{1}{2}$ cup peeled and grated carrots
  $1\frac{1}{2}$ teaspoons chili powder
  1 teaspoon ground cumin
  3 cups cooked pinto beans, drained (2 cans, 15 ounces each)
  2 tablespoons mustard
  2 tablespoons soy sauce
  2 tablespoons ketchup
  $1\frac{1}{2}$ cups rolled oats
  Salt and pepper to taste

Preparation:
  1. Sauté onions and garlic in frying pan with oil for about 5 minutes until onions soften.
  2. Add carrots, chili powder, and cumin and cook on low heat for another 5 minutes.
  3. Mash beans in a large bowl.
  4. Add mustard, soy sauce, ketchup, and fried onions/carrots mixture to mashed beans.
  5. Stir in oats and add salt and pepper.
  6. Moisten your hands and form mixture into six 3- or 4-inch patties.

7. Lightly spray or oil a nonstick skillet.
8. Cook on medium-low heat for 5–8 minutes on each side.

SERVES 4–6

❧ ❧ ❧ ❧ ❧

Lensey Namioka

Dear Lensey Namioka,

Hi, my name is Pat, and I am a sixth grader. Before I read your short story, I hadn't been much of a reader. But now I read much more knowing that there are more humorous stories out there. While I was reading your story, "The All-American Slurp," I became more interested in reading stories that are funny. I'm not much of an adventure, mystery, or biography reader. I like the way you made the Lins clueless about American culture in "The All-American Slurp." I especially liked the part when the Lins brought the dining chairs to the buffet table. Something unique I found while I was reading about you is that you too grew up in China but then moved to America, not knowing the culture very well.

Mrs. Namioka, the reason I have written to you . . .

Pat Smith

❧ ❧ ❧

Dear Mrs. Waltz,

One of your students, Pat, wrote me to ask if I would contribute a recipe for a cookbook you're compiling. Pat said the proceeds from the sale of the book would be given to the Children's Literacy Foundation. It sounds like a good cause, and I'm happy to contribute the following recipe: Chinese Chicken Salad.

Sincerely,
Lensey Namioka

Recipe from Lensey Namioka . . .

Chinese Chicken Salad

Cooking Equipment:
Large saucepan
Cutting knife
Cutting board
2 small mixing bowl

Measuring spoons
Wooden spoon

Ingredients:

1 chicken breast (or 2 chicken hindquarters, i.e., legs)
1 tablespoon soy sauce
2 tablespoons oil (canola, corn, or peanut oil is okay, but sesame oil is best)
1 teaspoon sugar
1 stalk of green onion

Preparation:

1. Boil the chicken in enough water to cover. Breasts take about 25 minutes, but legs take a little longer.
2. Cool the chicken. Cut or tear the chicken into thin shreds, until the meat is from $\frac{1}{4}$ to $\frac{1}{2}$ inch wide. (Thinner shreds are more elegant)
3. Place chicken in small bowl and set aside.
4. Combine soy sauce, sugar, and oil, mix well, and pour over chicken.
5. Slit stalk of green onions down the middle and cut it into thin, 1-inch segments.
6. Add green onions to chicken mixture and toss well.

SERVES 2

Author's Remarks:

The salad is ready to eat. Save the chicken broth for something else; it's too good to throw away. If you wish, you can throw away the skin. The salad can be one of the courses in a Chinese meal, or it can be served as an hors d'oeuvre. By the way, the seasoning is only approximate, and the cook can add or subtract from the amount, depending on taste.

Dorinda Nicholson

Dear Dorinda Makanaonalani Nicholson,

Your book *Pearl Harbor Child* was amazing. I have read it over and over. I keep thinking of how hard it must have been for you! Your book gave me a great interest in learning about Pearl Harbor. I love the details of your story and I am impressed by how personal it all is. I have not read your second book yet but I look forward to it! Your book was the hardest to stop reading because it is so interesting. I also admire you because after your Pearl Harbor incident you won a hula dancing competition, which you wanted to do!

I am writing to you from my middle school in New Jersey. I am hoping you will send a recipe for a special fundraiser my teacher is working on. My teacher believes in everyone being able to read. Some kids in this part of the country don't even have books! I chose you because you seem like a very warm and loving person and you look like you would agree with a situation like this one . . .

Thomas Madden

∾ ∾ ∾

Dear Thomas,

I truly enjoyed your letter and also the illustrations. It always pleases me when I hear from a school where the book is being used and also enjoyed. You must have a wonderful teacher to encourage and excite you in working to help the Children's Literacy Foundation.

The following is a recipe that I use often because it always works and cooks while I am gone, and it is easy.

Since you want fifty authors, I wondered if you were doing fifty states, and I was to send a Hawaiian recipe. If this is so, will you e-mail me and I will send another recipe that is more typical of Hawaii.

Good luck to you and your class on your project.

Aloha,
Dorinda

Recipe from Dorinda Nicholson . . .

Never Fail Roast

Cooking Equipment:
Cutting knife
Cutting board
Roasting pan

Ingredients:
4–5 carrots, washed and peeled
3–4 potatoes, washed, peeled, and cut in half
1 can of undiluted cream of mushroom soup
Roast
1 package of dehydrated onion soup

Preparation:
1. Preheat oven to 300°.
2. Place carrots and potatoes in bottom of roaster.
3. Cover carrots and potatoes with a can of undiluted cream of mushroom soup.
4. Put roast on top of vegetables and cover roast with package of dehydrated onion soup.
5. Cover tightly and bake for 3–4 hours.
6. Bake at 250° if you will be gone all day.

SERVES 4

Author's Remarks:
This roast never fails, and it even makes its own gravy and is guaranteed to be tender. The great thing about this roast recipe is that because of the slow-covered cooking, you can use any kind of roast so I would use the least expensive one.

∾ ∾ ∾ ∾ ∾

Kenneth Oppel

Dear Kenneth Oppel,

Hi, my name is Dan and I am eleven years old. I love your books *Silverwing* and *Sunwing*, which I thought are both really good. I was amazed when I heard you wrote your first book at age seventeen. Wow! Were you a talented writer in school? I thought it was interesting that *Colin's Fantastic Video Adventure* was a bestseller in three countries. When I went to your Web site I found out that Roald Dahl helped get your first book published. So your screenplays have been optioned by people in Hollywood? Congratulations! To tell you a bit about myself, I love to read novels that are fast paced and are always making the reader think. This is why I love the way you write your stories. I am a big fan of your books.

I really enjoyed *Silverwing* and *Sunwing* as I said before. I like the main character Shade because I think I'm a little like him. Do you ever think that when you write? I think the plots of your books are great. You really open the reader's mind to what it must be like to try to find something when the odds are against you. I felt bad for Shade in the first book because he was the runt of the colony and was always being picked on. When he was lost and found Marina, who was banished from her own kind, I was angered at the thought. The whole concept of the metallic bands and humans meaning something is a very unique idea. I thought *Sunwing* was amazing because you had the time set during a war and the bats and others get caught in the middle of it. The part I really like was at the end, when the owls and the bats make a truce. These are two of the best books I've ever read, and I cannot await the arrival of *Firewing* . . .

Dan Utkewicz

∾ ∾ ∾

Dear Dan,

First of all, please excuse the lateness of this letter. My publisher sometimes takes a very long time to forward my fan mail to me!

I'm so glad you've enjoyed *Silverwing* and *Sunwing*. A lot of people are curious about how I got interested in bats. Once I started reading about them, I realized what fascinating animals they were, and I was particularly interested in the idea of a migration—a long, difficult journey to escape the winter. Then I wondered what would happen if a young bat got lost on his first migration; how would he ever find his way? Would he have some kind of map? Would he have someone to help him?

I really wanted to invent a whole night time world for the bats—one where sound is as important as sight, with different laws, and different forms of technology and magic. Bats really do have "sound sight" or echolocation, but I invented the notion of sound maps sung from one bat to another, and the echo chamber, but they didn't seem too farfetched to me! And all my characters are based on real types of bats—even Goth and Throbb! Shade's a silver-haired bat; Marina's a red bat; Goth is something called a spearnosed bat, also known as the Vampyrum Spectrum. (Zotz is based on a real Mayan bat deity of the same name.)

I also wanted to pick names that seemed appropriate for flying creatures. So I used the names of some angels (Cassiel, Ariel), the names of special winds (Zephyr, Chinook, Scirocco—you can look them up!) and mythic heroes (Icarus). As for Shade, his name just reminded me of shadows and twilight. Marina means "of the sea"—she lives on an island as the story begins. And Goth is kind of shorthand for the word "gothic"— which conjured up all sorts of images of vampires and dungeons.

Right now, I'm writing the third book in the Shade saga, called *Firewing*. I don't want to give too much away, but much of the book will take place in the Underworld of Cama Zotz. One of the main characters will be Griffin, the child of Shade of Marina . . . and you haven't seen the last of Goth either! *Firewing* should be out sometime in Fall 2002. [Now published.]

Your recipe book sounds terrific. My wife is the chef at our house, so I don't do a whole lot of cooking. But one of my favorite dishes would have to be spinach lasagna.

Good luck.

Thanks again for writing!

Best wishes,
Kenneth Oppel

Dear Kenneth Oppel,

My name is Adam. I am twelve years old and was born in 1988 and have light skin and bluish eyes. I enjoy fantasy the most out of all kinds of books. I loved *Silverwing* and used it for a project. Next I read the sequel *Sunwing*. I thought it was wonderful and did a project on it also. I was disappointed that the great story came to an end there, but I was glad for it changed me in many ways. It taught me about bats in a great novel with Shade and Marina. It also told me to never give up even when your mission seems impossible. Being small as I am it taught me that size does not matter. I loved that you started writing young and have done so well in writing your books. I love your books very much and would like to learn a little about you . . .

Adam Stager

∾ ∾ ∾

Dear Adam,

Thanks very much for your letter. One of your classmates also wrote me about your recipe project and I have sent him one of my favorite recipes. You are welcome to use it in your book. It sounds like a very worthwhile project.

Check out my Web site at www.kennethoppel.ca for more information on me and my books.

Thanks again for writing!

Best wishes,
Kenneth Oppel

Recipe from Kenneth Oppel . . .

Spinach Lasagna

Cooking Equipment:

Cutting knife
Cutting board
2 large saucepans
Wooden spoon
Mixing bowl
13×9×2-inch glass baking dish
Aluminum foil

Ingredients:

1 package lasagna noodles
1 medium onion, chopped
1 pound lean ground meat
1 29-ounce can tomato puree
2 tomatoes, diced
1 package sliced mushrooms
1 teaspoon basil
1 teaspoon oregano
1 10-ounce package frozen spinach
1 16-ounce container cottage cheese
1 12-ounce package mozzarella cheese, shredded
Salt and pepper to taste

Preparation:

1. Preheat oven to 350°.
2. Cook lasagna noodles or use precooked kind and set aside.
3. Sauté chopped onion and brown lean ground beef in a large saucepan.
4. Add tomato puree, diced tomatoes, mushrooms, basil, and oregano and simmer for 20 minutes.
5. Cook, drain, and cool spinach, and combine with cottage cheese.
6. Place a layer of noodles at the bottom of baking dish.
7. Add a layer of meat sauce and then cottage cheese and spinach mixture.
8. Cover lightly with shredded mozzarella cheese.
9. Repeat layer of lasagna noodles, meat sauce, spinach mixture, and mozzarella cheese.
10. Repeat step 9 until all ingredients are used up and you reach the top of the baking dish.
11. Cover with aluminum foil and bake for 40 minutes.
12. Uncover and bake until hot and bubbly.
13. Let stand 10 minutes before cutting.

SERVES 8

Author's Remarks:

I start out by making a meat sauce with the above ingredients, but you can add whatever else you like in your meat sauce. Also, some people like to put a tomato sauce on top. I like a layer of meat sauce and mozzarella cheese on top. Then I cover it with aluminum foil so it doesn't dry out or frizzle up on top.

Philip Pullman

Dear Philip Pullman,

I enjoy reading your action packed books and hope you write more. *The Golden Compass* is my favorite out of your books because it is interesting and suspenseful. I have one brother, two parents, and a dog. I like to read fantasy books with nonstop mystery and suspense in them, which is why I love your books. You are by far my favorite author and you will be for a time to come. No one comes close to writing as good as you . . .

Andrew Zoller

Dear Philip Pullman,

I read your book *The Golden Compass* and the rest of your fantastic trilogy. I bought all three of your books because I was greatly moved by your work. I especially liked the ending to the trilogy. I like fantasy and action, and your book was perfect for me! I loved reading about Iorek and his adventures, and about Will's knife. I love your books and your wonderful characters (Will, Lyra, Lord Asriel) and your style of writing. I am definitely looking forward to reading more of your books . . .

Joel Shapiro

Dear Philip Pullman,

I have read *The Golden Compass* and enjoyed it very much. I particularly liked *The Subtle Knife*. I like the creativity in your books, like the way you created *dæmons*. My reading class is working on a project to get the favorite recipes of our favorite authors. If we get enough of them we will publish them in a cookbook. All the money will go to shelters and children . . .

David Holcomb

Dear Andrew, Joel, and David,

You've all written to ask me for my favorite recipe. Since I only have one favorite, there's no point in writing three letters back, so you'll have to share this one.

My greetings to Mrs. Waltz. Is she going to test all the recipes?

With best wishes.
Yours sincerely,
Philip Pullman

Recipe from Philip Pullman . . .

Chicken and Pancetta

Cooking Equipment:
>Large frying pan
>Large baking dish
>Measuring cup
>Measuring spoons
>Cutting knife

Ingredients:
>4–5 chicken breasts (one per person)
>Thin slices of pancetta or bacon (2–3 slices for each piece of chicken)
>Juice of a freshly squeezed lemon
>1 cup white wine
>1 or more tablespoons oregano, optional
>1 or more tablespoons parsley, optional

Preparation:
>1. Preheat oven to 350°.
>2. Wrap chicken breasts in thin slices of pancetta.

3. Fry chicken until golden, then place in baking dish.
4. Squeeze lemon juice over chicken, add white wine and herbs.
5. Bake for 1 hour or less, until juices run clear.

SERVES 4–5 PEOPLE

Author's Remarks:
You can use ordinary bacon but pancetta is best. I like to serve this dish with some green beans and rice.

∾ ∾ ∾ ∾ ∾

Mary Rodgers

Dear Mary Rodgers,

Hi, I'm April. When I read your book *Freaky Friday,* I absolutely loved it! From the first paragraph I read I knew I would enjoy the story. I thought I'd write a letter to you to explain why I loved your book so much and why I'm such a big fan of your writing.

I liked your book very much for various reasons. I liked the comedy that you put in throughout the book. I liked the main plot of the story, and it is a fun book to read. You were very descriptive about the characters and what they look like. For example, when you described that the character had brown hair, and brown eyes, and brown fingernails and that the character was five feet tall, but didn't remember how much she weighed, but that she was watching.

I think it's so neat that your father is Richard Rodgers! I am a very big fan of his! I absolutely love Rodgers and Hammerstein shows! I did a summer conservatory at the Paper Mill Playhouse this past summer for gifted and talented singers, dancers, and actors. (I love to sing.) And the show was a compellation of all Rodgers and Hammerstein shows. My favorites are *The Sound of Music* and *The King and I*. And I also understand that you write plays and compose music. I enjoy writing songs and I love to act (not as much as singing, but I love to act). Do you like to sing, act, and dance as well as write plays and compose? I find it very inspiring to have read a book that I enjoyed so much and then find out that we have a lot of the same interests . . .

April Bender

∾ ∾ ∾

April!

What a great letter! Are you sure you're only in the sixth grade? You sound much more grown-up than that.

I love your illustrations, especially the musical ones, and I'm intrigued by your participation in the Paper Mill summer program. Do you want to be in theater? I think we could use you!

Anyway, here's my favorite recipe. I've been using it for over fifty years—minus the garlic because not everyone likes garlic. (My father hated it.) If you're weight-conscious, you can use nonfat or low-fat yogurt instead of the sour cream, or a combination of both.

Oh, and when you first brown the meatballs, do them very quickly under very high heat and remove them when they're still quite pink in the middle. Then when you reheat them you'll be finishing them up rather than overcooking them. And they freeze, too. When you've defrosted them, add a little more sour cream.

Okay. That's enough cooking. I hope you like the two *Freaky Friday* sequels, too.

Best love,
Mary Rodgers

Recipe from Mary Rodgers . . .

Belgian Meatballs

Cooking Equipment:
Mixing bowl
Frying pan or skillet
Measuring cups
Measuring spoons
Saucepan

Ingredients:
2 pounds ground veal
1½ teaspoons salt
2 beaten eggs
½ cup milk
1 cup fine breadcrumbs
¼ teaspoon pepper
4 tablespoons oil
3 tablespoons minced onion
4 tablespoons flour
1 cup sour cream
1 tablespoon Worcestershire sauce
1 3-ounce can sliced mushrooms, undrained
4 cups uncooked broad noodles
3 tablespoons poppy seeds

Preparation:
1. Mix veal, salt, beaten eggs, milk, breadcrumbs, and pepper.
2. Shape into balls.
3. In skillet, brown meatballs in hot oil and remove when cooked.
4. Sauté onion in remaining oil in skillet 3–4 minutes.
5. Stir in flour, sour cream, Worcestershire sauce, and mushrooms.
6. Cook, stirring frequently until mixture thickens and ingredients are well blended.
7. Add meatballs to skillet while turning to coat them with sauce.

8. Refrigerate 6–8 hours.
9. Reheat meatballs and sauce over low heat.
10. Cook noodles. Drain and place them in a ring on a large plate. Add meatballs and sauce in the center.
11. Sprinkle with poppy seeds.

SERVES 6–8

Author's Remarks:
To tell if meatballs are done, cut into one of them with a sharp knife, then moosh it back together again.

Brad Strickland

Dear Brad Strickland,

Hi, how's it going? My name is Courtney and I'm a huge fan of yours. I have always loved to read and have been through a lot of books. When I first picked *The Vengeance of the Witchfinder* I thought it would be a pretty corny book. But when I got done with the first chapter, my eyes were glued to the book. Up to now, I have read the book a total of 5 times! I know how John Bellairs passed away in 1991, but I didn't know that until a few months ago when I finally read about the author. It really saddened me until I found out that you have been finishing his work! That got me jumping out of my seat! I have a few questions. About where did you pick up and finish his book? Were you and Mr. Bellairs friends before you finished some of his book? I loved how in the novel *The Vengeance of the Witchfinder* that you really brought out and back the characters. Even though I did, did you feel like you didn't have to read the other books to know the characters? Usually in sequels the characters are badly shaped but in this one they're brought back with a whole new life to them! When I read your book I felt enchanted by it. I loved the way how the whole plot of the story took place so nicely without any confusing ideas mixed in with it. I think you're so great because you took the liberty to finish John Bellairs' work. Also, you are truly an excellent author! Are you working on any other books?

Mr. Strickland, I'm not only writing this letter to you for a reply back (which is a treasure for life) but to also ask a favor . . .

Courtney Brownstein

Dear Courtney,

Thanks for writing to me. (You mailed the letter back on February 7, but I just got it today!) I'm sorry it's taken so long for me to reply, but my publisher sends me mail only a couple of times a year, so please forgive me for being so late.

I'm glad you liked *Vengeance of the Witchfinder*. That was a hard one to write, because when John Bellairs passed away, he had written only the first two chapters. His part ends just as Lewis catches sight of Barnavelt Manor. John had left little plot sketches for two other books, but there was nothing for this one, so I just had to make up a story that went with the opening. Mine begins on the first page of chapter three, and the rest of the book is mine. I also wrote *When Mack Came Back* and forty-nine other books, including many in the series of mysteries begun by John Bellairs. Some of these include *The Specter from the Magician's Museum, The Wrath of the Grinning Ghost,* and *The Tower at the End of the World.*

I am working on more books. There's a new Lewis/Rose Rita adventure that will be out in the summer of 2003 called *The Whistle, the Grave, and the Ghost.* That one's already turned in. (has been for months, but it takes a long time for a book to go through the publishing stage). [Now published.] Also, with my occasional co-writer Thomas E. Fuller, I've done a series of three pirate adventure novels, *Pirate Hunter,* that will be published beginning next November by Aladdin Books. The three books are *Mutiny! The Guns of Tortuga,* and *Heart of Steele* (Jack Steele is the evil pirate in the books). [Now published.] After that, I am writing a series called *Grimoire* for Dial books and one called *Mars: Year One* for Simon and Schuster. [Now published.]

Now, when you asked me for a recipe, the only thing I can think of is Fergie's favorite food from the *Johnny Dixon* stories: a big, juicy hamburger. I'll tell you the secret of my mouth-watering grilled hamburgers for the cookbook! I love them myself, especially when cooked on an open grill.

Thank you very much for offering me the chance. Best wishes to you for the rest of the school year, and I hope you have a great summer.

All best,
Brad Strickland

Recipe from Brad Strickland . . .

Best Big Bertha Burgers

Cooking Equipment:
Large mixing bowl
Measuring cups
Measuring spoons
Large nonstick pan

Ingredients:
1 pound lean ground beef or ground chuck
¼ cup breadcrumbs
¼ cup grated Parmesan cheese
¼ teaspoon black pepper
½ teaspoon salt
1 tablespoon Worcestershire sauce
2 tablespoons melted margarine (or butter if you don't mind the extra fat)
4 large hamburger buns

OPTIONAL TOPPINGS:
> Cheese
> Sliced tomato
> Lettuce
> Sliced or chopped onion
> Pickles

Preparation:
1. Prepare grill with help from an adult.
2. As the coals are heating, combine the meat, breadcrumbs, Parmesan cheese, pepper, salt, Worcestershire sauce, and 1 tablespoon of the melted margarine in a large bowl.
3. Using your fingers (be sure to wash your hands thoroughly before *and* after this step!), mix the ingredients together.
4. Be careful not to moosh the meat up too much. Shape into four large hamburger patties, approximately ¾ inch thick.
5. Grill these as you would an ordinary hamburger.
6. As the patties are nearing the end of their cooking, spread the other tablespoon of margarine in a large nonstick pan.
7. Grill the hamburger buns in the margarine until they're nice and toasty.
8. Serve up the patties on the buns.
9. Add whatever optional ingredients you like: cheese, sliced tomato, lettuce, sliced or chopped onion, pickles, and so on.
10. Spread the buns with mustard and/or ketchup and/or mayonnaise if you like.

SERVES 4

Author's Remarks:
I like mine medium-well done, nice and brown on the outside and cooked all the way through. These burgers will stay juicy even if they're well done, though, as long as you don't get them *too* well done.

   For exotic touches, try unusual toppings. I like grilled mushrooms, black olives, and even cole slaw now and again. These are great as Italian burgers, too, with zesty tomato sauce and some pizza seasoning. I even know one strange person who likes them with mayonnaise and sliced pineapple. But I don't think even Fergie, from the *Johnny Dixon* series, would go that far. Bon appetit!

Dave Wolverton

Dear Dave Wolverton,

   I am Tyler and I think you are a great author and I love your book, *The Rising Force,* which is part of the *Jedi Apprentice* series. My favorite part of the book was in the beginning when Obi Wan Kenobi is fighting Bruck Chun with the training sabers. This is because I did not know what was going on and I had to find out what was happening. This was my favorite book and I have read some of the other ones. I realized that most of them are by Jude Watson. I think you and she have the same style of writing. I have read all the books in this series up to number six. I have looked in lots of bookstores but I only found books that were from nine and up. I want to read them in order because it is one long story and makes more sense if you read them in order.

In your book, I liked how you described everything clearly so I can picture exactly what is going on. Sometimes I have to use my imagination but that is half the fun of reading a fiction book. I also like how unexpected things happen like when Qui-Gon Jinn met Obi Wan on that strange planet. These are all things I admire about the book but my favorite part is how there are many things in it that people today only dream about like light sabers and space ships traveling the galaxies at light speed. After I read the first chapter of this book I was amazed at the technology and how they took it for granted . . .

Tyler Luckewicz

ဆ ဆ ဆ

Dear Tyler,

I'm delighted that you liked the *Star Wars* novel. Here is my favorite recipe, one that I developed myself, Dave Wolverton. I hope you and your teacher like it.

Best,
Dave Wolverton

Recipe from Dave Wolverton . . .

Star Wars: Jabba the Hutt's Curried Pork

Cooking Equipment:
> Large frying pan
> Cutting knife
> Cutting board
> Wooden spoon
> Measuring cups
> Measuring spoons
> Saucepan

Ingredients:
> 2 pounds of thick-cut pork chops
> 2 tablespoons cooking oil
> 1 small white onion, chopped into small pieces
> 1 tablespoon butter
> 3 stalks of celery, chopped
> 1 apple chopped into small pieces
> 1 banana cut into small pieces
> ½ cup water
> ½ cup milk

Salt and pepper
¼ teaspoon ginger
2–6 tablespoons curry powder
¼ cup brown sugar
3 tablespoons flour
2 cups brown rice
1 package of shredded coconut
1 can of peanuts
1 bottle of peach-mango chutney

Preparation:

1. Fry pork chops in oil, then cut into small pieces about 1-inch square. Discard the bones and set cubes aside.
2. Fry onion in butter, browning all pieces.
3. Add celery, apple, banana, and water and cover and simmer until apples and bananas get soft.
4. Add milk to mixture and sprinkle a dash of salt and pepper.
5. Stir in ginger and 2–6 tablespoons of curry powder (2 for mild curry, 6 for hot).
6. Add brown sugar and flour and stir well to make curry gravy.
7. Add in pork cubes and simmer for 10 minutes.
8. Cook brown rice as per directions on the package and drain.
9. Pour the curry mixture over the cooked rice.
10. Serve with condiments of coconuts flakes, peanuts, and chutney.

SERVES 4–6

Author's Remarks:

I hope you and your teacher like it!

8 ✣ Desserts

T. A. Barron

Dear T. A. Barron,

First and foremost, I would like to compliment you on your magnificent novel *The Lost Years of Merlin*. I truly believe that I was meant to read it after nearly pulling down an entire shelf of books and was only able to catch one, which was none other than *The Lost Years of Merlin*. Being the tales of King Arthur fan that I am, this book suited my style of reading perfectly. From the instant that I read the first page I was blown away by the powerful writing and how it somehow tied in perfectly with the future of Merlin's life. It was almost the missing link to his past and it could not have been explained better. From his life in our world into the land of Fincayra, the good and the evil from the giants to even a small one like Shim, this book was by far number one on my list of favorite books.

To tell you the truth, I have read a lot of books. Before I get too carried away with the story, I would like to introduce myself. I am currently a sixth-grade student. I believe that my town is a great one; it's not too big but is very populated. The only problem is that it doesn't have enough forest. I read on your Web site that you like to go hiking in the mountains near your home. I also enjoy spending time in what forests we have that haven't been cut down yet. I believe that it is nice to be able to relate to your past and not keep concentrated on the future because fate plays its role to a certain extent. After all, humans didn't come into life with the luxury that we have today. Because you happen to be my favorite author I chose to write to you. The reason I write to you is that our reading class has come up with the most extraordinary idea . . .

Brian Keegan

༄ ༄ ༄

Dear Brian,

Thank you for your wonderful letter! I am delighted that *The Lost Years of Merlin* was so much fun for you. I hope you will enjoy the remaining four books in the story just as much; but it's best to read them in order if you can—*The Seven Songs of Merlin* is next.

Of course I would be happy to contribute my favorite recipe to your book! What a fun idea. My recipe is simple, and my sweet tooth is clear: Call it T. A. Barron's Amazing Ice Cream Feast, if you like. Although this is a simple dessert it is the best dessert I've ever eaten.

I love your illustrations—especially the marvelous tree. I think your thoughts about forests are very wise. Trees are truly our friends—if we don't destroy them. That's why I wrote *The Ancient One,* which is all about a great and wise tree that is also a time tunnel.

Best wishes to you—and your teacher, Mrs. Waltz.

Sincerely,
T. A. Barron

Recipe from T. A. Barron . . .

Amazing Ice Cream Feast

Cooking Equipment:
> Bowl
> Metal spoon
> A major sweet tooth

Ingredients:
> Häagen-Dazs Coffee Ice Cream (lots and lots!)
> Several graham crackers
> One cup of fresh-fallen snow

Preparations:
> 1. Warm ice cream to a soft consistency.
> 2. Put a large blob of ice cream into a bowl.
> 3. Crush several Graham crackers over the top.
> 4. Gently sprinkle snow over everything.
> 5. Then dig in!!

SERVES 2

ى ى ى ى ى

Clair Bee

Dear Clair Bee,

I enjoy your books more than any other author I have read in my twelve-year life. I especially enjoy *No-Hitter* very much because of the cultural enrichment you get with reading the book, not only the information and action about baseball. My favorite part from that book was when the character said he would pitch against Waseda. That was my favorite because that means that the whole problem of the story is solved. Tamio can now pitch for his native Japan team.

I am a reader that likes a quiet atmosphere to enjoy my book, do you? I enjoy sport books, especially baseball, my favorite sport. I know you were involved in basketball and baseball through your life too. How was that?

In class one day, my classmates and I were thinking of ways that their favorite author could connect to them in a special way . . .

Zach O'Connor-Robol

ى ى ى

Dear Zach,

Thank you most sincerely for inviting us to participate in your authors' cookbook; you and your classmates certainly arrived at a great approach for connecting all of us! Food possesses universal appeal!

My father, Coach Clair Bee, originally wrote the *Chip Hilton Sports* series for the 1940s to the 1960s. Before he died (in 1983), we promised Dad we would get his wonderful stories out to share with another generation of readers—you!

We are enclosing a brochure and a few *Chip Hilton* bookmarks for you that we thought you might like.

Since you mention *No Hitter* in your letter, we'd like to share some background with you. My father traveled to Japan in the early 1950s and was so interested in the Japanese people and their culture that he set *No Hitter* in Japan. In updating his books, my husband and I were able to add the Korea visit; Mr. Farley and I lived and taught in Seoul, South Korea, for three years. We were fortunate to attend the 1988 Olympics and also became friends with the coach and athletes on the South Korean Olympic Tae Kwon Do team. Our son was incredibly blessed to train with them. We now live in Indonesia.

Now—to Clair Bee's favorite recipe and a brief story that accompanies it! When my parents married, Dad told Mom he loved chocolate cake. For years, my mom baked him a wonderful, rich devil's food cake. However, one day Mom felt like baking something different. She decided on a white cake with chocolate icing. When Dad took his first bite, his eyes lit up and he pronounced, "Now *that's* a chocolate cake!" His definition and my mom's definition of a chocolate cake had certainly varied! The cake Mom baked on that day and for years and years after was a snow cake with chocolate icing— *exactly two* pages from the recipe she had used all those years to make her chocolate cake.

Zach, thank you again for including Clair Bee in your project and especially for the kind things you had to say about the *Chip Hilton Sports* series and *No Hitter*.

Work hard, read widely, and stay true to your ideals.

Sincerely,
Cynthia Bee Farley and Randy Farley

Recipe from Clair Bee . . .

Snow Cake with Milk Chocolate Frosting

Cooking Equipment:
8-inch cake pan
Electric mixer
Small mixing bowl
Large mixing bowl
Measuring cups
Measuring spoons
Saucepan or double boiler

Ingredients:

CAKE MIXTURE:
3 egg whites
1 cup sugar
½ cup butter
1½ cups flour
2 teaspoons baking powder
¼ teaspoon salt
½ cup milk
½ teaspoon vanilla

MILK CHOCOLATE FROSTING:
2 squares milk chocolate
1 tablespoon butter
½ cup milk
2–3 cups confectioners' sugar
½ teaspoon vanilla extract

Preparation:

CAKE MIXTURE:
1. Preheat oven to 350°.
2. Grease and flour cake pan.
3. Beat egg whites until stiff, stir in half the sugar, and set aside.
4. Cream butter and gradually add remaining sugar while beating constantly.
5. Sift flour, baking powder, and salt and mix alternately with milk.
6. Fold in beaten egg whites and stir in vanilla.
7. Pour batter into cake pan and bake for 45 minutes.

MILK CHOCOLATE FROSTING:
1. Combine chocolate, butter, and milk in a saucepan or double boiler and cook over low heat, stirring frequently.
2. Once chocolate has melted, remove from heat and let stand until mixture is lukewarm.
3. Add vanilla extract and then gradually add confectioners' sugar and beat until mixture is of the right consistency to spread.

SERVES 6–8

Andrew Clements

Dear Andrew Clements,

I am a big fan of your style of writing. Oh, by the way, my name is Ryan. I am in sixth grade. Last year I read the two most amazing books I have ever read. Those books were *Frindle* and *The Laundry News*. In *Frindle* you created happiness between all of the characters except for the teacher, but in the end you made her character develop into a pleasant and good-natured person. And in *The Laundry News* the kids made up a newspaper and people actually read it. When this happened it made me feel happy inside because the kids got looked up to as the cool kids. People in my school don't really see me as the kid who did something great. I think you are the best author because you create humor and it's actually funny. You know, some other authors try to say something funny but then it's not that funny, you know what I mean?

When I was reading your biography I realized that you wrote poems and song lyrics. What kind of poems did you write? What types of songs did you write, slow or fast? Did your parents write songs? Back to the poems, did you ever get any of them published in books? Not only am I writing to tell you how good an author you are, I would like to know what your favorite recipe is? My teacher will ask if she can put it in a book for a children's literacy foundation. This foundation is for children and libraries who don't have a lot of books . . .

Ryan Van Splinter

ꙮ ꙮ ꙮ

Dear Ryan,

Thank you for your kind letter—sorry for the delayed response.

Recipe from Andrew Clements . . .

Penny's Brownies

Cooking Equipment:
9-inch square baking dish
Saucepan
Mixing bowl
Eggbeater
Wooden spoon
Measuring cups
Measuring spoons

Ingredients:
Butter for greasing pan
1 stick of butter
3 squares of chocolate
2 eggs
1 teaspoon vanilla
1 cup sugar
½ cup flour

Preparation:
1. Preheat oven to 325°.
2. Grease baking dish.
3. In a saucepan, heat butter and chocolate squares over low heat until melted and set aside.

4. Beat eggs, vanilla, and sugar.
5. Pour melted chocolate mixture into beaten egg mixture.
6. Stir in flour until all ingredients are well blended.
7. Spread mixture evenly in baking dish and bake 20–30 minutes or until a wooden toothpick comes out clean.

SERVES 4–6

Author's Remarks:
Yum!

∾ ∾ ∾ ∾ ∾

Jane Leslie Conly

Dear Jane Leslie Conly,

My name is Brent. I am a sixth grader. Usually when I pick up a book I put it back down. I am a very picky reader. The book has to spark my interest in a special way. That is why I think you and your father are the two greatest writers that have ever published a book. All three of the NIMH books were extremely well thought up and interesting. I also think that it was interesting that your father made his pen name Robert C. O'Brien.

When I read *Mrs. Frisby and the Rats of NIMH* for school, I couldn't put it down. Each day I read more and more. After a few days, I had finished the book. What I then thought was the greatest book of all time was about to change.

At that time I was so far ahead of my class that my teacher let me read *Rasco and the Rats of NIMH*. In *Rasco and the Rats of NIMH,* Timothy and Rasco are such strong characters. They also both come from totally different places. The way you have them meet and learn to cope with each other makes them such good role models for me and other children. They teach us to accept people who are different from us. With Timothy as a farm boy and Rasco a city boy, Timothy has to teach Rasco the ways of life in the wilderness . . .

Brent LaMaire

Dear Jane Leslie Conly,

Hi! My name is Raymond. I am eleven years old and I like to play sports, especially baseball. I have a mother, a father, and two younger brothers. When I read I like to read your books.

I love reading your books and the books that your father wrote. You are my favorite author and I love your series. My favorite book was *Mrs. Frisby and the Rats of NIMH* that was written by your father. I like how the smallest mouse gets sick and how the smart rats and the owl work together to save him. Also, I like the characters and how they have to go through many events to reach their goal of moving Mrs. Frisby's house. It is my favorite because it shows that you can't judge someone on how they look, like the rats in *Mrs. Frisby and the Rats of NIMH*. This is why you are my favorite author and why I love your books.

You are my favorite author. I have researched and found out many things about you. First, I think it is great that you like to fish. Second, I think that it's also great that you work as a director at a community center and it is also great that you own a log cabin in southern Pennsylvania. Lastly, I think it's cool that you lived on a farm when you were a kid and that you got a degree from Smith College . . .

Raymond Menzel

ॐ ॐ ॐ

Dear Brent and Raymond,

Thank you for the wonderful letters. I'm sending a recipe that has been a favorite of my mother's. It was served every Christmas.

Sincerely,
Jane Leslie Conly

Recipe from Jane Leslie Conly . . .

Date Nut Tort

Cooking Equipment:
Sifter
Small mixing bowl
Medium mixing bowl
Measuring cups
Measuring spoons
Whisk
Wooden spoon
9-inch pie pan

Ingredients:
$\frac{1}{2}$ cup flour
1 teaspoon baking powder
$\frac{1}{8}$ teaspoon salt
$\frac{3}{4}$ cup sugar
3 eggs
$\frac{1}{2}$ teaspoon vanilla
$1\frac{1}{2}$ cups chopped dates
$1\frac{1}{2}$ cups broken nuts (walnut or pecan)
Whipped cream

Preparation:
1. Preheat oven to 325°.
2. Sift and combine flour, baking powder, and salt and set aside.
3. Beat sugar into the eggs, then stir in vanilla, dates, and nuts.
4. Add dry ingredients to wet ingredients and mix well.

5. Pour batter into pie pan and bake for 50 minutes or until firm.
6. Cool and serve with whipped cream.

SERVES 4–6

∾ ∾ ∾ ∾ ∾

Anne Fine

Dear Anne Fine,

Your book *Charm School* made me remember exactly what it was like when I moved to different countries. I didn't know if I'd make any new friends so I wanted my old ones back.

My name is Brittany and I'm in the sixth grade. I have just moved from Belgium, though I had only lived there for three and a half years. I am originally Australian. I love it here in the U.S. and everyone is really nice. Have you ever moved to different countries before?

I loved the book *Charm School* because I thought that it was very realistic, I mean this is a thing that happens for a lot of kids who are Bonnie's age; everything in life changes. I also liked this book because it shows that everyone is different and also has a sense of humor. This book was really interesting and it made me want to read on. I think you are a great author and you are one of my favorites. Even though I read this book in early fifth grade, I still like to read it now.

While I was researching you, I learned that you didn't just write for kids, but that you wrote for adults as well. Which ones do you prefer writing for? I also learned that you did very well in school, especially university! Did this help you at all with your writing? I learned that you very briefly taught in a Scottish prison. I found that very unique and interesting. About how long were you there and what sort of things did you teach . . .

Brittany

∾ ∾ ∾

Dear Brittany,

Yes, you certainly do sound a *mover*. I stayed in England as a child though we did move. But my daughters were in schools in England, Scotland, Canada, California, Arizona, and Michigan, so they certainly knew how it felt. When the oldest was eleven, we settled down, for her sake, till they both finished school.

But it sounds as if things have worked out well for you.

I hope you'll try some of the other books. You can't get all of them in the States. But Amazon is always there.

It was so nice of you to write. Here's the recipe. Fax copy so don't get it wet.

Love,
Anne Fine

Recipe from Anne Fine . . .

Toasted Grapes and Cream

Cooking Equipment:
   4 pudding dishes with straight sides
   Cutting knife
   Cutting board

Ingredients:
   1 pound or more chilled grapes
   Large, chilled carton of heavy whipping cream
   Dark brown sugar or Muscovado sugar

Preparation:
   1. Cut grapes in half lengthwise and remove any large seeds.
   2. Divide the grapes into four individual pudding dishes.
   3. Pack down with double cream to within a half inch of the top and chill.
   4. Then pack a quarter inch layer of brown sugar over the top and return to the refrigerator.
   5. Just before serving put pudding dishes under a broiler for 1–2 minutes, until bubbly and spitting.

   SERVES 4

Author's Remarks:
   Eat carefully. The cream and grapes stay cold, but the top can burn your mouth. Delicious!

Johanna Hurwitz

Dear Johanna Hurwitz,

   Hi! My name is Neela. I am eleven years old and go to middle school. I am one of your *biggest* fans. Although I have read one of your books, *The Hot and Cold Summer,* I enjoyed it a lot. I have to say, I have read that book about ten or twenty times. I don't call myself much of a reader but I think your book is exceptionally good. In the novel, *The Hot and Cold Summer* I have to say my favorite part is when Bolivia, Derek, and Rory are playing with snowballs, or should I say ice-cream balls?! Your book is so good that I remember myself laughing aloud many times. In addition, I think you are very descriptive with your work and I feel I am right there in the book. In addition, I admire how you incorporate real life into your work. You are my favorite author because you make children who do not like reading want to read. You are one of the people that I will always look up to. As I was researching you, I found out that as a young child you wanted to become a librarian. My mother is a librarian and

I like to work with her. In addition, I read that you wanted to be a writer. How did you make your dream come true? I am writing because my teacher has a project in which I need your help . . .

Neela Kumar

∞ ∞ ∞

Dear Neela,

Thank you for the lovely letter that you sent me. I'm glad to know you have read and enjoyed *The Hot and Cold Summer*. That's the best news an author can get. Books and reading have always been important in my life. I can remember my parents reading stories aloud to me when I was young. I was very excited when I joined the public library and could borrow books and bring them home to read. When I was your age, I began writing my own stories and even asked a girl in my class if she would illustrate one for me. However, it took until I was a grown woman until my first book, *Busybody Nora*, got published.

The ideas for my books come from everywhere: memories of my childhood, events that happened to my children when they were growing up, articles I read in the newspaper, things I see out of the window. Even my cats gave me ideas for my stories.

In all, I have written sixty-four books. Some are about Aldo, others are about Lucas Cott, Cricket Kaufman, Ali Baba Bernstein and Rory, Derek and Bolivia who have adventures every season of the year, and many other characters. I've also written a few nonfiction books—biographies of people who really lived like Astrid Lindgren and Helen Keller. My next book will be coming out in October. It's called *Fourth Grade Fuss!* [Now published.]

Everyone always wants to know which is my favorite book. It's much too difficult for me to select one. However, it's possible that you'll have a favorite.

Happy reading and happy all year long.

Your friend,
Johanna Hurwitz

P.S. Look in your school or public library for *The Cold and Hot Winter*, *The Up and Down Spring*, and *The Down and Up Fall* to learn more about Rory, Derek, and Bolivia. Here is a recipe for your collection. I can't say it's my "favorite" one because I know so many. However, since I've written *Aldo Ice Cream* and *The Hot and Cold Summer* (with the chapter featuring an ice cream snowball fight), I thought it would be appropriate to share a recipe for homemade ice cream. Good luck!

Recipe from Johanna Hurwitz . . .

Lemon Cream Sherbet

Cooking Equipment:
   Measuring cups
   Blender
   Grater
   Small mixing bowl

Metal spoon
Quart-sized container for freezing

Ingredients:
2 cups heavy cream
¼ cup plain yogurt (unflavored)
1 6-ounce can frozen lemonade concentrate—do not add water
½ cup granulated sugar
Pinch of salt
Grated rind of 2 lemons

Preparation:
1. Measure all ingredients except lemon rind and pour directly into blender.
2. Add grated lemon rind, cover, and blend for 2 minutes.
3. Pour blended mixture into a freezer container and freeze for several hours or overnight.
4. Remove from freezer about 20 minutes before serving to soften.

MAKES 1 QUART

Author's Remark:
Be sure and share it with others. Don't eat it all yourself! Enjoy!

Eva Ibbotson

Dear Eva Ibbotson,

I loved your book, *The Secret of Platform Thirteen*. I enjoy reading your books because of the way they are brilliantly put together. One thing happens and a new event follows right behind it. Just like every nine years, a portal opens to get from one world to another. Then a prince becomes stolen and you send four opposites to find him. You really capture a different world that a reader never usually discovers. How do you research for a story like *The Secret of Platform Thirteen*? What inspired you to write a book like this? Whatever or however you write, you do a great job!

I have a request . . .

Hilary Giunta

Dear Hilary,

Your letter reached me last week! Letters do take a long time to reach me, partly because, as you see, I live in England, and partly because publishers do not always send on letters as quickly as they might. I'm really sorry you've had to wait so long for my reply.

The Island in *The Secret of Platform Thirteen* is based on a beautiful island off the west coast of Scotland, which I used to go to for holidays when I was a child. It's just a speck on the map, but it has everything you could dream of—white sandy beaches, every kind of sea bird, and seals that used to come and watch us swim. When I wanted a magical island, it seemed to be the perfect place to use. I've used it in *Island of the Aunts* as well. Once a place gets into your imagination it stays there, as I'm sure you know. I find it best when one is writing fantasy to use a familiar place and then put in the imaginary creatures—the mist makers and hags and harpies.

I think compiling a recipe book with author's favorite foods is a very good idea. I've chosen a Sacher torte because I was born in Vienna, Austria, and it's practically the national dish. It's named after Herr Sacher, who is supposed to have invented it, though there is a lot of argument about this and the head baker at Demels said *he* invented it and they nearly came to blows. But this was long ago.

It's very fattening but I'm afraid people in Vienna didn't bother much about calories or being thin. My great aunt Bertha was so fat that she went through doors sideways!

I wish you all the best for your project.

Yours sincerely,
Eva Ibbotson

P.S. The recipe came from my grandmother.

Recipe from Eva Ibbotson . . .

Recipe for Chocolate Glaze supplied by J. Waltz.

Sacher Torte

Cooking Equipment:
9-inch deep round tin cake pan or 9 × 2.5-inch springform pan
Double boiler or saucepan
2 mixing bowls
Measuring cups
Measuring spoons
Food processor for grinding almonds
Wooden spoon
Metal spoon
Eggbeater or electric beater

Ingredients:

CAKE MIXTURE:
8 ounces cooking chocolate
1 tablespoon water
2 sticks butter
8 eggs separated
1 cup ground almonds

¾ cup caster sugar
1 tablespoon corn flour
Apricot jam or sauce (hold for later)

FILLING:
4 egg yolks
¼ cup sugar
¼ cup cocoa
½ cup double cream
2 tablespoons vanilla sugar

CHOCOLATE GLAZE:
½ cup sugar
¼ cup water
5 ounces chocolate
¼ teaspoon melted butter

Preparation:

CAKE MIXTURE:
1. Preheat oven to 300°.
2. Grease and flour pan.
3. Melt the chocolate with 1 tablespoon of water and set aside.
4. Cream butter, add melted chocolate, beaten egg yolks, ground almonds, and sugar, then beat all ingredients until very light and creamy.
5. Add corn flour to batter, beat again, and set aside.
6. In a separate bowl beat egg whites until peaks form, then fold into batter.
7. Transfer batter to pan and bake for 1 hour.
8. Leave torte in pan to cool thoroughly before turning out.

FILLING:
1. Cook the beaten egg yolks, sugar, and cocoa, stirring until mixture thickens, and set aside to cool.
2. Whip double cream, then add vanilla sugar, and fold into cooled cocoa mixture.
3. Cut cooled cake in half and spread the lower half with chocolate filling.
4. Replace top half of cake and spread a thin layer of warm sieved apricot jam or sauce.

CHOCOLATE GLAZE:
1. Dissolve sugar in water, stirring frequently over medium heat, and set aside.
2. Melt chocolate over low heat until soft.
3. Stir lukewarm sugar into melted chocolate.
4. Stir in melted butter until well blended.
5. Spread a thin layer of chocolate glaze over cake.
6. Serve with whipped cream.

SERVES 6–8

Author's Remarks:
Makes you very fat!!

Paul Jennings

Dear Paul Jennings,

Hello my name is Thomas and I liked *Uncanny* so much and it touched me and it was the greatest book. Your books are so unique and so interesting that I can't stop myself from reading more. My favorite character in any of your books would be Jack Thaw, he is so *cool* and interesting that I was wondering how you came up with the character? Also, your stories are so well written that I felt like I was actually there and amazed by seeing a cow on the street. Also, I felt I was in the story when Guts Garvy stole that remote from the kid, I was so mad at Guts. I think you are the greatest author because you know how to write so that people really listen and are moved by your works. I also have read all the books of yours that start with the prefix *"Un."*

When I was researching you for this letter, I found out that you like classic cars. I think this is great because I like classic cars too. *Je t'admire** because it takes a lot of persistence to fix up a car and make it nice. It is also interesting that you like to show your cars at clubs. I also know a place near my house that once a week has classic cars at their place. My dad and I sometimes go and it is really nice looking at the classic cars.

Not only have I written to tell you how much I enjoy your writing, but to ask a favor of you . . .

Thomas Woodford

*I admire you (In French).

∾ ∾ ∾

Dear Thomas,

Thanks for your letter and the lovely things you have said about my books. I am sorry it has taken me so long to reply to your letter. I have been away promoting my new book, *The Reading Bug,* and am only just catching up on all my correspondence. I have enclosed a copy of my favourite recipe—Bread and Butter Pudding.

At long last we have moved into our new home. I am very excited by this move because I will be able to sit in my new study watching the ocean as it foams and crashes about me. In winter I will be able to watch the whales. There is also a cave nearby and lots of wild beaches and cliff tops to roam along. I think that I will get a lot of inspiration for my stories in this magic place.

Tongue Tied seems to be going well. I had a great time writing this collection of short stories, especially the title story: *Tongue Tied*. Imagine walking around with a goldfish in your mouth!

I get many letters asking me about myself and my family so I've come up with a booklet that will hopefully answer everyone's questions and it also includes writing tips for enthusiastic young writers. Many people ask me, 'Will you come to our school?' I worry that they will think I'm mean for saying 'no' but I'd never have time to finish another story if I did.

Thanks again for writing to me. When I think about it, it's a great life being a writer. I wouldn't want to do anything else. My dreams came true—I hope yours do too.

Best wishes,
Paul Jennings

Recipe from Paul Jennings . . .

Bread and Butter Pudding

Cooking Equipment:
Butter knife
9-inch baking dish
Small mixing bowl
Saucepan
Eggbeater

Ingredients:
Butter
4 slices white bread (crusts removed)
$\frac{1}{4}$ cup sultanas
$1\frac{1}{3}$ cups milk
$1\frac{1}{3}$ cups cream
1 vanilla pod (or $\frac{1}{2}$ teaspoon vanilla extract)
3 large eggs
$\frac{1}{2}$ cup caster sugar

Preparation:
1. Preheat oven to 325°.
2. Spread butter generously over one side of bread slices.
3. Place bread in a greased ovenproof dish with buttered side up.
4. Scatter the sultanas over the bread.
5. Boil milk and cream, then stir in vanilla.
6. Let mixture stand for 10–15 minutes.
7. Beat eggs into sugar, add milk mixture, and stir well.
8. Pour mixture over the bread and sultanas.
9. Bake in a water bath until set.

SERVES 6

∾ ∾ ∾ ∾ ∾

Wil Mara

Dear Wil Mara,

Hello, my name is Christina, and I am in the sixth grade. I love your book *What's Up with the New Principal?* I usually say things like I don't like this book, or it's too boring after the first chapter, though when I read the first page of your book, I knew I was going to love it. One specific thing that I loved was the prank that Mike had made up about Mr. Collins' car. I could really picture it in my mind! Also, the way Mr. Collins always reads the book on how to be a good principal. I can't believe how you can make such good ideas for your stories and still make them realistic so everyone could relate to it. Especially when Lisa finds out that the new principal is not that bad when he helps her with math. I know that everyone thinks one person is bad, but when they really get to know them they prove themselves wrong. That was cool because you made the fight between the characters, thinking Lisa was betraying them, so suspenseful. I really don't know that much about books, though after reading your book, I can pick out main events and understand some of the harder things like comprehension. When I read your book I felt many things. For example I felt so excited when Mike, Lisa, and all the others were setting up pranks like the spiders, and also, the tension between characters when Brian bumped into the new principal the first day back to school. I love your book very much, and truly think you are very talented the way you wrote the story.

The most important reason I am writing to you . . .

Christina Gilhuley

ᘉ ᘉ ᘉ

Dear Christina,

Thank you for your wonderful letter concerning my novel *What's Up with the New Principal?* I was very flattered (to the point of embarrassment, actually) by all your kind words. I had a lot of fun writing that book. I have often wondered if youngsters who read it would want to start playing practical jokes on their own principals. I don't recall playing any on mine when I was in elementary school. Then again, maybe I did and I'm just not *choosing* to remember. I'll have to ask my mom about that.

Anyway, you asked for a recipe. Hmm . . . well, there are lots of great recipes. I could've suggested twenty as easily as I could've suggested one. I doubt, however, that would've helped you very much. So I narrowed the list down to two, both of which are attached to this letter. If you feel neither is quite right, let me know and I'll submit some more. I think this cookbook project of yours is marvelous, by the way—you and your classmates should be very proud—and I am honored to be a part of it.

And again, thank you for your letter. It was greatly appreciated.

Best wishes,
Wil Mara

Recipe from Wil Mara . . .

Classic Strawberry Scones

Cooking Equipment:
Cutting knife
Cutting board
Bowl
Wooden spoon
Fork
Rolling pin
Cookie sheet
Small bowl

Ingredients:

DOUGH:
    1 cup strawberries
    2½ cups flour
    4 tablespoons sugar
    2 teaspoons baking powder
    Dash of salt
    6 tablespoons butter
    ⅔ cup of milk

TOPPING:
    1 cup heavy cream
    ¼ cup sugar
    1 teaspoon vanilla extract

Preparation:
    1. Preheat oven to 425°.
    2. Dice strawberries and set aside.
    3. In a bowl mix dry ingredients.
    4. Add butter and blend everything until crumbly.
    5. Stir in strawberries, toss, and then add milk.
    6. Mix with fork until it holds together.
    7. With floured hands, form dough into two balls.
    8. Roll on floured surface into two circles, each ½ inch thick.
    9. Cut each circle into triangular slices (like a pizza).
    10. Place on greased cookie sheet and bake for 10–12 minutes (or until golden brown).
    11. While scones are baking, whip the cream, sugar, and vanilla extract in a cold bowl until stiff (the mixture, not your arm).
    12. Serve warm with whipped cream.

Choconut Ice Cream

Cooking Equipment:
    13×9×2-inch freezer container
    Measuring cups
    Metal spoon
    Saucepan
    Long heavy knife

Ingredients:
    1 pound chocolate sandwich cookies, crushed
    ½ cup margarine, melted
    1¾ cups confectioners' sugar
    1 12-ounces can evaporated milk
    1 cup semisweet chocolate chips
    ½ cup margarine, *not* melted
    1 teaspoon vanilla extract

½ gallon vanilla ice cream
1½ cups regular or dry-roasted peanuts

Preparation:
1. Combine crushed cookies and melted margarine, press into a large, shallow dish, and chill for an hour in refrigerator.
2. In a saucepan over medium heat, combine confectioners' sugar, evaporated milk, chocolate chips, and margarine.
3. Bring chocolate mixture to a boil, stirring frequently for 8 minutes.
4. Remove from heat, stir in vanilla, and set aside to cool.
5. Divide vanilla ice cream into ¾-inch slices, then place slices in a single layer over chilled crust.
6. Smooth seams and sprinkle peanuts over the ice cream.
7. Top with cooled chocolate sauce.
8. Cover and freeze eight hours (overnight).

James Vance Marshall, a.k.a Donald Payne

Dear James Vance Marshall,

Hello, my name is Michael. I am twelve years old with a family of four. I live in New Jersey along with some of my close friends. I have lived here most of my life and I enjoy it very much. I am currently reading your book you wrote, *Walkabout,* and I love it. This book is filled with wonderful descriptions of the Australian landscape. If you have visited this place, please tell me more in a different letter. I look forward to reading the rest of your works . . .

Michael Humbert

Dear Michael,

Thank you very much for your letter about *Walkabout,* a story that I wrote more than forty years ago in collaboration with the late James Vance Marshall. The enclosed two pages from the publishers guide *Latitudes* explains how the book came to be written.

I am so glad you enjoyed the story and am very flattered that you say I am your favourite author.

I am happy to "Donate a Recipe"—this is enclosed.

May I congratulate you and your reading teacher Mrs. Waltz on what sounds a very worthwhile idea. I wish your project every success and you yourself every happiness.

Yours,
Donald Payne

Recipe from Donald Payne . . .

Recipe supplied by Donald Payne's daughter-in-law, Kathie Payne of Melbourne, Australia.

Fruit Dish Pavlova—an Australian/New Zealand Dish

Cooking Equipment:
Whisk or electric mixer
Measuring cups
Measuring spoons
Large bowl
Wooden spoon
Baking tray
Silicone baking paper or nonstick cooking spray

Ingredients:
4 egg whites
½–1 cup white sugar
1 teaspoon corn flour
1 teaspoon white vinegar
1 teaspoon vanilla extract
1 cup whipping cream
8 ounces bite-sized pieces assorted fruit (strawberries, raspberries, passion fruit, mangos, and kiwi)

Preparation:
1. Move oven rack to lowest position.
2. Preheat oven to 300°.
3. Take a baking tray, turn it upside down, and cover it with silicone paper or nonstick spray.
4. Beat egg whites until stiff and gradually add sugar until well blended.
5. Quickly add corn flour, vinegar, and vanilla extract, then turn mixer off at once.
6. Make a flat circle with about half the mixture, then heap the other half around the edge leaving a hollow in the center.
7. Place pavlova in oven, immediately turn oven to 200°, and bake for 90 minutes.
8. When cool, fill hollow with whipped cream and fruit.

SERVES 4–6

Author's Remarks:
The eggs should be at room temperature, not straight from the fridge, before they are whipped. Make sure all utensils are dry before using.

∾ ∾ ∾ ∾ ∾

Phyllis Naylor

Dear Phyllis Naylor,

   Hi, I'm Amanda. I'm eleven years old and I've read all the *Shiloh* books and they are great. First let me say that I wasn't going through the bookstore and I picked up your book *Shiloh*. In fourth grade my teacher read it to us because she had said it was one of her favorites. When she finished reading it to us in her Southern accent I loved the book so much I bugged my mom to get it for me. I really like the fact that your book is about a boy who wanted this dog so much he would offer to work for Judd, this horrible man, who in the end didn't even give him the dog (who was so useless for him). The part of your story that I really liked was the fact it is all about a dog (which is my favorite animal next to the horse). Plus the fact that I'm a little like Marty, I'm like him because he begged and begged for Shiloh, just like me, for I want a dog more than anything. So I can relate to Marty. As odd as it seems Judd was one of my favorite characters (Shiloh the first) because he mistreated Shiloh and made the story more exciting and Shiloh more important to be saved by Marty. Though it's odd, Judd makes the story a lot more interesting. I was wondering if you put him in the story so Marty could have a better reason to save Shiloh?

   I also like to write about many things as long as I don't have a deadline. Do you like the deadlines the publishing company gives you? I think that it's odd that now you are such a wonderful writer but as a child you had troubles in reading. I think it is very interesting that you didn't finish college and went to writing full time. One other thing I think is amazing about you is how you can write for six hours a day . . .

Amanda Richelo

❧ ❧ ❧

Dear Amanda,

   I'm so glad you liked the *Shiloh* books. You were wondering if I put Judd in the story so Marty could have a better reason to save Shiloh. If Judd wasn't in the book, there wouldn't be much of a story at all! I'm afraid you're mistaken about college: I did finish, but I didn't major in cooking, as you will see from my recipe. I'm not much of a cook because I would rather write than anything else I can think of.

My very best wishes,
Phyllis Naylor

Recipe from Phyllis Naylor . . .

Strawberry Orange Toast

Cooking Equipment:
   Cutting knife
   Cutting board
   Measuring cup
   Measuring spoon

Grater
Small mixing bowl
Small cookie sheet

Ingredients:
2 English muffins
Butter
1 tablespoon freshly grated orange peel
$\frac{1}{4}$ cup sugar
1 cup fresh or frozen strawberries, sliced
Whipped cream

Preparation:
1. Preheat oven to broiler.
2. Slice each muffin to make 4 halves.
3. Butter each muffin half.
4. Mix grated orange peel with sugar and sprinkle over muffin halves.
5. Place muffins on cookie sheet and broil until lightly browned.
6. Put strawberries and whipped cream on top.

SERVES 4

❧ ❧ ❧ ❧ ❧

Robert Kimmel Smith

Dear Robert Kimmel Smith,

Hi, my name is Joe. I would like to talk to you about your book called *The War with Grandpa*. Some of the things that I liked about the novel *The War with Grandpa* is that you could understand why Peter was mad at his parents and played tricks on his grandpa. The idea that the grandfather could play tricks like that was also enormously hilarious. Peter didn't get into trouble either. I felt sorry for Peter's grandfather because he had arthritis in his leg and couldn't walk well and then his wife died and all this caused him to become very depressed. I particularly liked your writing because it was very comprehensible and easy to understand. It was also very clear why Peter and his grandfather were playing tricks on each other. What I didn't understand was why Peter had been that mean to take his grandfather's teeth, though. That was the only part I didn't like and it was definitely my least favorite part.

I think that it was amazing that your book *The War with Grandpa* got 11 state awards, especially when you got 5 of them in 6 weeks. I was also surprised to find out that you could write a story just from your son saying he loved his house and his room.

I also heard about the joke you wrote and got it published when you were a little kid. That shows how talented you were even when you were young . . .

Joe Greco

❧ ❧ ❧

Dear Joe,

I loved your letter. Glad you liked the book. Keep your eye on the ball and your nose in a book.

Your friend,
Robert K. Smith

Dear Robert Kimmel Smith,

Hi, my name is Caity, and I'm in the sixth grade. One of the first books I read when I was younger was *Chocolate Fever*. I loved it so much, I read it over and over, until I almost memorized it word by word. When my teacher saw this she suggested that I read more of your books—so I did.

I thought the cover of the book you wrote was eye-catching, because of all the candy, and details swirling around his head. Also, when Henry's parents just laugh about his love for chocolate. I think it's funny that they just go along with him, and keep letting him eat chocolate with everything. Personally, I don't like chocolate that much, but I thought it was a little gross that Henry has chocolate with everything, but it was still pretty creative. Even with dinners! My parents would never let me have candy with all my meals—or anything else . . .

Caity Law

❧ ❧ ❧

Dear Caity,

Thanks for your sweet letter. I'd be glad to send you a recipe of mine. I do love chocolate a lot, so it's for my *Chocolate Fever Brownies*.

Your friend,
Robert Kimmel Smith

Recipe from Robert Kimmel Smith . . .

Chocolate Fever Brownies

Cooking Equipment:
Saucepan
Measuring cup
Measuring spoon
Eggbeater or electric mixer
Mixing bowl
8×8-inch baking pan

Ingredients:
Crisco
1 stick butter
3 squares unsweetened chocolate

1 cup sugar
2 eggs
¾ cup flour
¼ teaspoon salt
¼ teaspoon baking powder
1 teaspoon vanilla extract
6 ounces semisweet chocolate chips

Preparation:

1. Preheat oven to 350°.
2. Grease 8 × 8-inch pan with Crisco.
3. Melt butter with unsweetened chocolate squares over low heat and let cool.
4. Add sugar, eggs, dry ingredients, and vanilla extract, beating until smooth, then fold in chocolate chips.
5. Pour into baking dish and bake for 29 minutes.

Author's Remarks:

You'll get a fudgy center with lush chips. They can be cut and wrapped in foil. Frozen. Good out of freezer. Guaranteed to give you *chocolate fever*! (*Oh,* no!)

$\backsim \backsim \backsim \backsim \backsim$

Jerry Spinelli

Dear Jerry Spinelli,

Hi, my name is Frank and I'm in sixth grade. I read your book *Wringer* a while ago and I really enjoyed reading it. I felt really relaxed while reading this book, yet I was very into it. Reading your book was like being in my own miniature world. I especially liked the part when Farquar gives Palmer the treatment, and how you build up all the suspense during that part. That is one of the reasons why I like your writing. Your writing can be funny or suspenseful—anything you want it to be—and it's always entertaining.

What I think is interesting about you is that you get your ideas from the kids. I think that you can really learn a lot from us and that you show that in your writing. Do you always write about kids in your novels? You definitely can turn an ordinary kid like me into an interesting character . . .

Frank Cui

Frank,

Here's a recipe. The card is for you.

Jerry Spinelli

Recipe from Jerry Spinelli . . .

Thelma's Chocolate Cake

Cooking Equipment:
   Large mixing bowl
   Measuring cups
   Measuring spoons
   Saucepan
   Wooden Spoon
   Electric beater
   Tube pan

Ingredients:
   2 cups flour
   2 cups sugar
   2 teaspoons baking soda
   4 squares chocolate
   ½ pound butter
   1 cup water
   2 eggs
   1 cup sour milk
   1 teaspoon vanilla

Preparation:
   1. Preheat oven to 350°.
   2. Mix flour, sugar, and baking soda and set aside.
   3. Heat chocolate, butter, and water over low heat until melted.
   4. Add chocolate mixture to dry ingredients and stir well.
   5. Beat eggs, milk, and vanilla and stir into mixture until smooth.
   6. Pour in tube pan and bake for approximately 1 hour.

SERVES 6–8

ᐤ ᐤ ᐤ ᐤ ᐤ

Cynthia Voigt

Dear Cynthia Voigt,

My name is Frannie, and I just recently read your novel *Homecoming*. It was one of the best books I have ever read! I have read other books of yours, such as *Izzy Willy Nilly* and *The Runner,* both of which I enjoyed. But *Homecoming* is just such an intensely terrific read; I could barely put it down. In fact, it was so good, it is the book I am doing for the meeting of my book club.

The reason I liked *Homecoming* so much was because everything was so realistic and down to earth, not having everything happy and perfect, it felt like real life. It was shocking to me when the Tillerman's mother just . . . walked away. It made me feel angry that she could just leave her children like that, as if she didn't care about them. I read later on that she was in a mental institution, but I was still angry she left them. Loving your children should be everlasting love, and you shouldn't just leave them, no matter how hard life is.

I also thought it was kind of the baker in the story to give them so much food when they didn't have enough money left to buy anything, and they were on the point of starving. I don't think that would have actually happened today, but it was a good thing they needed the push to give them hope to go on. I thought the best part of the story was when the Tillerman's went to live with their grandmother, and she hated them. But Dicey never gave up. She kept on annoying Abigail Tillerman into loving them and keeping them. I thought that showed a great amount of courage, and it was a wonderful ending.

Overall, I think this was a depressing novel, but still an incredible one. Sometimes I think you need to read a depressing slap-of-reality story to have it be a good one.

While I was researching up on you for writing this letter, I read that you decided to become an author when you were in the ninth grade. I thought this was really interesting, because I have wanted to be an author since I was seven. Did you ever think maybe being an author would not be the career for you? Up until fifth grade, I was sure I wanted to be an author. But now I am not so sure. I think a vet, or an environmentalist, or even a teacher would be fun! I also read you were a teacher, even though you vowed you never would be one. What made you decide to become a teacher? I think teaching fifth grade would be good to be able to learn what kind of books children like. I remember a lot of fifth grade was doing book reviews and reading novels . . .

Frannie Nicholas

∾ ∾ ∾

Hello Frannie,

And thank you for your letter. I am honored by your good opinion of my work. Sometimes, I would agree with you. More times, I keep thinking I can do better, do more, do differently, do . . . oh, I don't know, some mysterious thing that I can almost glimpse the shadow of on the distance horizon of my imagination. You know?

Anyway, I have a nit to pick with you about whether Momma would have walked away if she loved her children. You seem to think she wouldn't. But try this way of thinking about it: If she loved them deeply, and she could see herself collapsing mentally, what would be the best thing she could do for them? The most loving thing, I mean, as well as best.

About writing as a career, it seems to me that writing is something you can do along with many other things, almost any other thing. Time could be a problem—because being a vet, for example, takes a lot of time, or a teacher, or an environmentalist; however, if you make the time, there are vets and environmentalists and teachers who have written some interesting things. So I don't think you have to choose between writing and some other work. Try having both, why not be a little greedy about life?

On another page, I am including one of my favorite recipes, called Grammy's Hot Milk Cake. It's the first thing I ever cooked, and I've served it to happy eaters all of my cooking life.

Cynthia Voigt

Recipe from Cynthia Voigt . . .

Grammy's Hot Milk Cake

Cooking Equipment:
9-inch square cake pan
Large mixing bowl
Eggbeater or electric mixer
Measuring cups
Measuring spoons
Wooden spoon

Ingredients:
2 eggs, well beaten
1 cup sugar
1 cup flour
1 teaspoon baking powder
$\frac{1}{2}$ cup scalded milk with butter—a piece the size of an egg, 2 ounces—melted in it
1 teaspoon vanilla extract

Preparation:
1. Preheat oven to 350°.
2. Grease a square cake pan and lightly dust with flour.
3. Beat sugar into eggs.
4. Add flour and baking powder and beat well.
5. Stir in scalded milk and melted butter mixture, then stir in vanilla extract.
6. Pour batter into greased pan and bake for about 30 minutes.
7. Frost by sifting confectioners' sugar over cake while it is still hot in the pan.
8. Cut into squares or bars to serve.

SERVES 6–8

Author's Remarks:

Variations: Use cake flour for a finer grain. Flavor with both 1 teaspoon vanilla extract and $\frac{1}{2}$ teaspoon Almond extract. Double the recipe and cook in a bundt pan.

∾ ∾ ∾ ∾ ∾

Lance Walheim

Dear Lance Walheim,

Hi, my name is Jared and I'm eleven years old. Your book, *Vegetable Gardening,* is my favorite book. I especially like the descriptive and educational A to Z encyclopedia. Reading your book inspired me to start my own vegetable garden, which is what I am in the middle of doing right now. I think you are a great author because of how descriptive you are. Also, because you are smart and give step-by-step instructions on what to do. I want to read your other gardening books so I can learn more about gardening. I think that is very special how you are sharing your gardening skills with other people around the world. I have two questions. What inspired you to write all of your gardening books, and do you have your own garden?

Now that I told you that you are a great author and that I love your books, maybe I should tell you a little bit about myself. I enjoy fishing, gardening, and collecting baseball cards. I am not much of a writer, but I love to read books like yours. . . . Until June . . .

Jared Reichenberg

∾ ∾ ∾

Dear Jared,

Thanks so much for your letter. I don't get letters that nice every day. I think I'll frame it.

I'm glad you like my book. I've enclosed a little bio of myself so you can see some of the other things I've written. Basically, I got a degree in botany from the University of California, Berkeley. When I got out of school, I was lucky enough to meet some people who were writing gardening books for Ortho. I had always loved growing plants and gardening with my father when I was young. Anyway, Horticultural Associates hired me to run their test garden in St. Helens, CA. Botany was a good basis for gardening but I had a lot to learn and the test garden was a great place to learn it.

Gradually I did more and more writing until I was assigned my own book, Ortho's *The World of Trees.* Since then I've worked a lot for *Sunset Magazine* and *Sunset Books* and written so many books I've lost count. I just finished working on a landscaping book for Lowes home stores.

I live in Exeter, CA, on a seventeen-acre citrus ranch where we grow specialty citrus like blood oranges, Meyer lemons, and Page mandarins. The recipe I'm including is for Meyer lemon sorbet. Meyer lemons might be hard to find in NJ, but ask your supermarket and maybe they can get them. If they can, they will probably come from my ranch. I do a lot of gardening and have a great vegetable garden. I also like to grow flowers, especially roses.

Here's something else you might be interested in. My brother Rex is an astronaut. He's going up in the space shuttle on April 4th. He's scheduled to do two space walks. Pretty exciting huh? Maybe you can watch the launch on TV.

Anyway, thanks again for your nice letter. Write me again if you get the chance.

Lance Walheim

Recipe from Lance Walheim . . .

Quick Meyer Lemon Sorbet

Cooking Equipment:
2-quart saucepan
Measuring cups
Wooden spoon
Grater
10-inch square metal pan
Metal spoon
Blender or food processor

Ingredients:
1 envelope unflavored gelatin
1½ cups Meyer lemon juice
¾ cup sugar
1½ cups water
3 tablespoons grated Meyer lemon peel

Preparation:
1. Pour unflavored gelatin, Meyer lemon juice, sugar, and water into saucepan.
2. Mix ingredients well and bring to a boil on high heat, stirring frequently.
3. Reduce heat and simmer for 5 minutes.
4. Add grated lemon peel.
5. Pour into pan and freeze until hard, approximately 3 hours.
6. Remove pan from freezer and let stand at room temperature until it can be broken into large pieces with a metal spoon.
7. Place the pieces in a blender or food processor and whirl until smooth and frothy.
8. Spoon into dessert dishes and serve immediately.

SERVES 4

∿ ∿ ∿ ∿ ∿

Jacqueline Wilson

Dear Jacqueline Wilson,

My name is Carlie and I'm a big fan of your books. Actually I've only read one of them and that's *Double Act,* but I plan to read many more since this one was so great. I was wondering how did you get your idea for a book about twin girls who are completely different? I found out that you actually wanted to be an author all your life. When did you first think of becoming an author, and who inspired you? I also found out that *Double Act* is going to be turned into a TV series. When will it be coming out? I really want to see it. I even saw that you are going to have a part in it. Who are you going to be? If you have time to read my letter and answer my questions, then please do so.

I also wanted to tell you what I liked about the book since it was so great. The first thing is that I loved what the book was about, twins. I really like those kinds of books. I also liked how you wrote the book so it seemed like you were reading it from the girl's diary. I liked when they tried out for the TV series. It was brave and pretty cool. The last thing that I really liked is when Rudy and the Blob became friends, and Garnet went to boarding school. That sounds like fun.

Remember the end of the book when Rudy cut her hair? I didn't think she would actually do it. I was so surprised when she just cut it all off. But I was also sad when Rudy got mad at Garnet for going to boarding school. Then at the very end I was very happy again when everything was the same between Garnet and Rudy . . .

Carlie Sanders

∾ ∾ ∾

Dear Carlie,

I'm so sorry, sweetheart, your letter has only just been sent onto me. Presumably it's much too late to include a recipe from me in your class special book. I'm a hopeless cook anyway, so maybe it's just as well! If by chance it's not too late then ask your mom for her favorite apple pie recipe, and that can be *my* choice.

I'm so glad you liked reading *Double Act.* It's already been on British TV—I don't know whether you'll get to see it in the states.

Love from,
Jacqueline Wilson

Recipe from Jacqueline Wilson . . .

Carlie's Mom's Naked Apple Pie

Cooking Equipment:
9-inch pie pan
Sifter
2 large mixing bowls
Measuring cups

Measuring spoons
Electric mixer
Cutting knife
Cutting board
Large spoon

Ingredients:

½ cup flour
1½ teaspoons baking powder
1 egg
½ cup brown sugar
1 teaspoon vanilla extract
Pinch of salt
2 large tart apples
½ cup chopped pecans

Preparation:

1. Preheat oven to 350°.
2. Grease pie pan.
3. Sift together flour and baking powder and set aside.
4. In a separate bowl, beat egg with electric mixer.
5. Add brown sugar, vanilla extract, and salt.
6. Beat mixture at medium speed for 1 minute.
7. With beater running, add flour mixture and beat until smooth.
8. Peel, core, and cut apples into thin slices.
9. Fold apples and nuts into batter.
10. Spoon into pan and bake for 30 minutes.
11. Cool completely and serve with vanilla ice cream.

SERVES 4–6

~ ~ ~ ~ ~

9 ❧ Cookies and Snacks

Meg Cabot

Dear Meg Cabot,

Hi, my name is Michele. I am writing to you because I am a huge fan of your book *The Princess Diaries*. The style of your writing in *The Princess Diaries* is my favorite. Reading is not really one of my favorite things to do but after I read your book that all changed. I couldn't put it down. I could definitely relate to Mia and so can many other girls my age. Like how she gets through some of the problems of being a teen and daughter of divorced parents. I know how she feels because I am a teen and a daughter of divorced parents. I think you have a great talent in describing the characters and events in your stories. Like when Mia first found out that she was a princess. Our class is on a mission . . .

Michele Billera

∿ ∿ ∿

Dear Michele,

I am ashamed of myself for having taken so long to reply to your nice letter. As you might know, my book became a movie this summer, and so things have been slightly hectic. But I am finally getting around to answering my mail, and I hope it is not too late for my recipe to be included. Also, Michele, I want to say thank you very much for reading my book, and I hope you will accept this signed copy as a token of my regret for not having answered your letter before you graduate or whatever.

I would have sent you the sequel, *Princess in the Spotlight,* but there appears to be a national shortage of that book at this time, so I have supplied a signed bookplate. In the event you ever do get your hands on a copy, you can stick this inside, and it will be like I signed it for you.

I hope you saw the movie and if so you did not hate it, as Disney is currently making a sequel.

Well, that is all. I am attaching my recipe. I hope this letter finds you and Mrs. Waltz well!

Sincerely,
Meg Cabot

Recipe from Meg Cabot . . .

Nestlé Toll House Break and Bake Chocolate Chip Cookies

Cooking Equipment:
Cookie sheet
Cooking spatula (a burger flipper thing)

Ingredients:

Butter
Nestlé Toll House Cookie Dough, precut squares kind

Preparation:

1. Preheat oven to 350°.
2. Grease cookie sheet with butter.
3. Break off squares of cookie dough.
4. Put squares you do not eat raw on tray, spaced about 2 inches apart if possible, unless you're making one giant cookie, in which case, place squares close together. (From my own experience, making one giant cookie is not advisable.)
5. Put cookies in oven and open oven door every 2–5 minutes until cookies look brown on top.
6. Remove tray from oven (wear an oven mitt while doing this).
7. Let tray sit and cool for no more than 3 minutes.
8. Remove cookies from tray with one of those burger flipper things.

Author's Remarks:

Enjoy warm, or, as I prefer, frozen. The perfect writer's snack!

Mark Crilley

Dear Mark Crilley,

My name is Julia. I am eleven years old and I am very interested in your books! I have been reading your books since fifth grade. One of your novels that I absolutely loved was your first one, *Akiko on Planet Smoo*. I am reading *Akiko in the Sprubly Islands*. My favorite parts in this novel are when the robots came by to Akiko's window in the floating car and they told her to get in. One other part that I like (I can't name them all, there are too many!) is when they are all fighting on planet Smoo with the T–Rex. When I was reading this I felt like I was a little kid again and I had the biggest imagination in the world and that I could do anything.

The reason that you are a fantastic author is because you write what the kids want to hear. Also, I think that you are a fantastic author because you make people have an imagination like when you imagine so much that you think that you are in the novel and one of the characters.

I think that it is amazing that ever since you could hold a pencil/pen in your hand you wanted to be a writer. I think that it is amazing because I have only met a few people that knew what they wanted to do when they were a kid. I wanted to be a couple of things when I grow up and one of those things is a writer but I don't know if I am ready yet.

About writing, one of the things that I love and that my reading teacher thinks that I am good at is poetry. I really like poetry because I think that it is fun to write and make it rhyme. Also, I love to make my poems funny. I am not only writing to tell you how much I love your writing, but to ask you for something . . .

Julia Povolny

∾ ∾ ∾

Dear Julia,

Thanks so much for your letter, and sorry for my unbelievably long delay in replying! There's simply no excuse. None that *I* can think of, anyway.

I'm so glad you like my *Akiko* books. It really means a lot to me to hear from a young reader like you. It reassures me that I'm reaching just the sort of person I wanted to reach with these books.

Thanks for taking the time to write your thoughts down and send them to me. I really do appreciate it.

Okay, here is my recipe. It's one I came up with myself, just by goofing around and experimenting. That's why the instructions are anything but accurate! So here it is . . . Mark Crilley's Darned Simple Date & Pecan Granola.

Well, there you have it! I hope this is the sort of thing you were looking for. Again, sorry for taking so long to reply to your letter. To make amends, here's a little drawing for you!

Best wishes,
Mark Crilley

Recipe from Mark Crilley . . .

Darned Simple Date & Pecan Granola

Cooking Equipment:
  Large, deep baking pan
  Small frying pan
  Measuring cups
  Wooden spoon

Ingredients:
  1 large 42-ounce container old-fashioned Oats
  1 cup and slightly more vegetable oil
  2 cups or more dates
  2 cups or more chopped pecans

Preparation:
  1. Preheat oven 350°.
  2. Pour oats in baking pan.
  3. Heat vegetable oil over medium heat for 5 minutes until hot but not "frying hot."
  4. Stir in hot oil a little at a time to coat oats.

5. Place pan in oven and bake for 20 minutes, stirring frequently.
6. Turn off oven and remove pan.
7. Stir in dates and pecans, then return pan to oven for 10–15 minutes to soften dates.
8. Remove and let cool. You're done!

MAKES 10 CUPS

Author's Remarks:

This recipe makes a whole mess of servings. If you like your granola sweet, try adding a little maple syrup at the end. But you've used loads of dates so this granola needs no added sugar at all.

ॐ ॐ ॐ ॐ ॐ

Dean Marney

Dear Dean Marney,

Hello, my name is Jennifer and I just love your books. I read *The Jack-O-Lantern That Ate My Brother* and *How to Drive Your Family Crazy on Valentine's Day*. They were very funny, interesting, and sometimes scary. I plan to read more of your books.

I liked the part where four people were gobbled up by a box in the *How to Drive Your Family Crazy on Valentine's Day*. They were unusual, hilarious, and amusing. The part when Elizabeth was trying to clean up the large stacks of dishes to find her brother but the dishes wouldn't go away and when she pulled the witches nose are my favorite parts from *The Jack-O-Lantern That Ate My Brother*. Most of all I liked the books because of Elizabeth. She is like me. She can't concentrate very well. She doesn't make friends easily. She and I have a younger sibling who is always annoying and gets into troubles. Except that I don't get the blame. I think it is wonderful to write and publish books. Writing fairy tales and fiction based on real life stories is very interesting. I need to ask a favor from you . . .

Jennifer Han

ॐ ॐ ॐ

Jennifer,

I'm sorry it took so long for me to answer your letter—thank you for writing to me. My recipe is from my book *Pet–rified*.

Thanks again.
Dean Marney

Recipe from Dean Marney . . .

No-Bake Cookies

Cooking Equipment:
Bowl
Measuring cups
Measuring spoon
Large saucepan
Wooden spoon
Metal spoon
Waxed paper

Ingredients:
3 cups quick oats
¾ cup coconut
½ cup nuts
¾ cup miniature marshmallows
2 cups sugar
½ cup butter or margarine
½ cup milk
2 tablespoons powdered cocoa

Preparation:
1. Mix quick oats, coconuts, nuts, and marshmallows in a bowl and set aside.
2. Combine and bring sugar, butter, milk, and powdered cocoa to a boil, then continue to boil for an additional minute.
3. Pour heated mixture over dry ingredients and mix well.
4. Using a spoon place cookie-sized drops on waxed paper and let cool.

MAKES 2 DOZEN COOKIES

Author's Remarks:
You've got yourself some No-Bake Cookies.

Marissa Moss

Dear Marissa Moss,

Hi! My name is also Marissa. I am a sixth grader and attend middle school in New Jersey. *Amelia's Notebook* and all other Amelia books were such wonderful and special books that I could not put them down. The drawings and little details written around the pictures were so terrific! I especially enjoyed the "Useful Information" in the back of the book where there were little comments written around the information. In addition, a book designed as a notebook is such a clever and unique idea and the character, Amelia, is someone just about every kid can relate to. Also, you give such humorous, original descriptions of each character (like that Cleo has a jelly roll nose!). As I was reading, I was amazed at how comical and realistic *Amelia's Notebook* was. I knew just by glancing at the first page that I wanted to read all the stories about Amelia! Reading all of *Amelia's Notebooks* is like reading the diary of someone my age; it's awesome! I have also read your book *Rachel's Journal*. This, too, was a wonderful piece of writing and a great way to learn and discover more about the past in a fun, enjoyable way. One specific thing I liked was the realistic drawings and captions. A couple of years ago, my reading teacher, Mrs. Waltz, decided to give her students a project based on your journals! She had her students write in a journal format (similar to the Amelia book) and include little illustrations and phrases around them. As you can see, all of your stories are terrific and I hope you create many more.

The reason I am writing to you is because of a project . . .

Marissa Tarabocchia

∾ ∾ ∾

Dear Marissa,

Great name! I'm embarrassed to say that I *just* got your letter. I'm sorry the publisher took so long to pass it on to me. Now I don't know if it's too late to give you a recipe. Just in case your teacher can use my recipe for next school year, I'll include one.

Anyway, I'm very sorry to be so late. I hope you weren't disappointed that I didn't answer sooner.

Your friend,
Marissa Moss

Recipe from Marissa Moss . . .

Chocolate Chip Peppermint Cookies

Cooking Equipment:
Cookie sheet
Electric mixer or fork
2 bowls
Metal spoon

Ingredients:
¾ cup butter or margarine (1½ sticks)
½ cup brown sugar
½ cup granulated sugar
1 egg

1 teaspoon vanilla extract
1 teaspoon peppermint extract
1½ cup white flour
1 teaspoon baking soda
¼ teaspoon salt
½–1 cup chocolate chips (judge for yourself how much is enough)

Preparation:
1. Preheat oven to 350°.
2. Lightly grease cookie sheet.
3. Cream together butter and both sugars (you can use an electric mixer or just a fork).
4. Beat in egg, then stir in vanilla and peppermint extracts.
5. In separate bowl, mix flour, baking soda, and salt, then add to butter mixture.
6. Stir in chocolate chips and mix well.
7. Drop by spoonfuls on cookie sheet and bake 12–15 minutes.

MAKES 2½ DOZEN COOKIES

෴ ෴ ෴ ෴ ෴

Bill Myers

Dear Bill Myers,

My name is Ben. I live in New Jersey. I love your books! I also enjoy sports. My favorites are basketball, skiing, and golf. I was originally born in Canada but moved here one year ago. My favorite book that you have written is *My Life as a Human Hockey Puck.* My favorite part is the beginning of the book when you were describing all different pains you can have. I also enjoyed the rest of the book. It was *hysterical!* Your *Bloodhound Inc,* series is great too! My favorite characters in those books are Slobs and Bears.

I am sure you will add to your trophy case more than the 40 awards that you have now if you keep on writing the way you do. I will look forward to your future books . . .

Ben Whitt

෴ ෴ ෴

Hey Ben,

Isn't school over? Well, in case you're going to (gulp) summer school or something, here goes: My favorite all-time food is Party Mix!

Bill Myers

Recipe from Bill Myers . . .

Party Mix

Cooking Equipment:
Saucepan
Measuring cup
Measuring spoons
Large bowl
2 or more 13×9×2-inch baking dishes

Ingredients:
1 large box each: Corn, Rice, and Wheat Chex cereals
2 containers Spanish peanuts, 3 pounds each
3 sticks butter or margarine
½ cup soy sauce
5 tablespoons Worcestershire sauce
¾ teaspoon garlic powder

Preparation:
1. Preheat oven to 175°–200°.
2. Melt butter over low heat, stir in all seasonings, and set aside.
3. Combine cereals and peanuts, then place in baking dishes.
4. Dribble melted seasonings over dry ingredients, mix well, and bake 6–8 hours.

MAKES ENOUGH PARTY MIX FOR A HUGE PARTY!

Note:
To reduce quantities try: 3 cups of each cereal, 1 or 2 cups Spanish peanuts, 6 tablespoons of butter, ½–1 tablespoon soy sauce, and 2 tablespoons Worcestershire sauce, bake at 180° for 1 hour, stirring every 15 minutes.

Author's Remarks:
Eat until you explode!

ფ ფ ფ ფ ფ

Barbara Robinson

Dear Barbara Robinson,

My name is Kevin and I am eleven years old. I am in the sixth grade. I have read your book *The Best Christmas Pageant Ever* and really enjoyed it. I have read a few of your other books also. But I especially liked *The Best Christmas Pageant Ever*.

I am writing to you because my reading teacher is having us work on a very special project. As part of the project I would persuade people to read this book by saying that this is a really funny book and that you should read it because it has some awesome passages. One funny part was when a character said they were glad to see the Herdmans but that it was really the biggest lie said inside a church.

We would really appreciate it if you helped us out and sent your favorite recipe to help some kids.

Thank you so much for taking your time to read this letter and I may send a few more to you over the years . . .

Kevin Leveille

∾ ∾ ∾

Dear Kevin,

Thank you for your letter. I'm sorry to be so late in answering, but I've been on vacation on Cape Cod (still am, in fact) and my mail has been greatly delayed! I'm so flattered that you've chosen me to be part of this special project. I hope that I'm not too late.

I'm sending you my favorite cookie recipe and I happen to know that it's also the Herdmans' favorite.

I said I'm on vacation, which is true, but authors rarely are on vacation. I'm finishing a new Herdman book in between swims and sails . . . hope you enjoy it, too, when it is done.

Thanks again, Kevin, for your letter, and for the enthusiasm you've shown about my books.

Sincerely,
Barbara Robinson

Recipe from Barbara Robinson . . .

Chocolate Wonders

Cooking Equipment:
    Double boiler or large saucepan
    Cookie sheet
    Wooden spoon
    Measuring cups
    Measuring spoons

Ingredients:
    1½ packages chocolate chips (9 ounces)
    1 tablespoon margarine
    1 14-ounce can sweetened condensed milk
    1 teaspoon vanilla
    1 cup flour
    ¾ cup chopped walnuts

Preparation:

1. Preheat oven to 350°.
2. Grease cookie sheet.
3. Melt chips and margarine over low heat or in a double boiler, stirring frequently.
4. Stir in condensed milk.
5. Stir in vanilla, flour, and nuts.
6. Drop by spoonfuls (sort of medium size) on cookie sheet and bake.

MAKES 2 DOZEN COOKIES

Author's Remarks:

You may use more or less walnuts to suit yourself. The time is up to you. 25 minutes—firm, chewy cookies. 10–15 minutes—soft cookies. The Herdmans, however, don't bake them at all. They drop the batter, by teaspoons, on a greased sheet . . . wait a while . . . sometimes half an hour even . . . and enjoy them as fudge . . . you can do that too!

ɷ ɷ ɷ ɷ ɷ

10 ∾ Additional Student and Author Letters

Eoin Colfer

Dear Eoin Colfer,

Hello! My name is Jasmine. I am in sixth grade and attend middle school. I loved the *Artemis Fowl* book that you wrote. You are truly one of my favorite authors. I'm interested in reading books that deal with magic and sorcery, and your book has all those characteristics. It's perfect for me! The way you make the reader wonder what will happen in the next chapter really keeps your readers involved. You build so much suspense throughout the book and your style of writing inspires me. You have so many incredible details in *Artemis Fowl* that I couldn't stop reading it. My parents had to come into my room every night at bedtime and tell me to stop reading your book.

I understand you are making a sequel? I can't wait to read it. I hope you have a wonderful time completing the sequel. I think that it's great that you're teaching children as well as writing your book! Also, I heard that Miramax is making a movie based on your book. I agree with you that the movie should be filmed in England and not in Hollywood. Movies based on books should be filmed in the country where the story takes place.

I know that you live in Wexford and wonder if it's pretty there? I live in the country where there are lots of horses, houses, and people. Could you please write back and tell me what the countryside is like? I hope to visit England sometime when I go on vacation with my family. My father travels to England occasionally for business and said he would try and take me with him on one of his trips. I would love to meet you in person and talk to you more about *Artemis Fowl*.

The main reason I am writing to you is to ask a big favor . . .

Jasmine Khadr

∾ ∾ ∾

Dear Jasmine,

My favorite dish is pepperoni pizza, which I get at a local parlor called Rebetinos—so I'm afraid I don't even have to cook it!

Sincerely,
Eoin Colfer

Dan Gutman

Dear Dan Gutman,

Hi, my name is Tim. I love the book you wrote *The Shortstop Who Knew Too Much*. I like the personality you gave Jake and how he got ESP by Whip hitting him with a baseball. I also liked how you made Jake have the ability to steal answers from people's heads. I like how you set the mood of anger when Whip called Jake on the telephone to apologize and Jake was mad at him for calling. I like the cheer about choppin them and sawen them and then sanden them! This story was fun to read because it had to do with baseball.

This story made me feel scared in the beginning when Whip hit him in the head. It made me feel happy when the team won a lot of games. It made my imagination wild when he could literally steal answers from people's heads. I think you are the best author because you write interesting stories and you put in *a lot* of details. When I read the book *The Shortstop Who Knew Too Much* I looked at the back of the book and it said you are a big fan of baseball. Who is your favorite baseball player?

Dan, I have six questions to ask you. Do you have any pets? I have two Bichon Poodles and two hermit crabs. What inspired you to write humor? Was it fun to write for computer magazines? How did you feel when your first paycheck was only fifteen dollars? Why did you move to New Jersey? The biography you wrote said you wrote for the magazines *Newsweek, Science Digest, Writers Digest, Success, Psychology Today, New Woman, U.S.A Today,* and *The Village Voice.* Which one was your favorite?

Not only did I write to my favorite author to say I love your books, but for you to think of your favorite recipe. My class would like to publish it and if we get any money, it would go to the Children's Literacy Foundation. This foundation is for libraries that don't have enough books . . . please know you have a *big* fan in New Jersey.

Tim Esposito

∾ ∾ ∾

Dear Tim,

Thank you so much for your wonderful letter. It is kids like you who inspire me to write my books. I'm not a famous author or anything like that, so it is that much more special to me when kids write me letters and tell me they enjoy my work. I wish I could contribute a recipe for your book, but I just don't know how to cook. Sorry.

Right now I'm in the middle of a book about Benjamin Franklin. But I wanted to take a few minutes to answer your questions: My favorite baseball player is Mike Piazza. I have one cat, named Scrumpy. I always liked reading funny books, so I guess that made me want to put humor in my stories. No, I did not like writing for computer magazines. I was *thrilled* when I got that first check, even though it was small. I have lived in New Jersey almost my whole life.

Thanks for reading *The Shortstop Who Knew Too Much.* If you want to find out about my other books, stop by my Web site (www.dangutman.com).

Until then, I leave you, hoping you'll read lots of books, whether they're mine or somebody else's (but especially mine!). Because the more you read, the more you know.

Cheers,
Dan Gutman

P.S. Say hi to the kids for me! And tell them to read my books! I need more fans like you!

Richard Peck

Dear Richard Peck,

Hi, my name is Dana. My hobbies include writing poems, biking, swimming, and dancing. I was born in New Jersey and still live there, so I guess you can call me a Jersey girl. I live with my mom and sister Kerri. In my lifetime I would love to become a famous chef, and publish cookbooks, and an autobiography. Your books have become a household favorite.

Many students now are very strong readers that hated reading, but that's not me. I would say I'm an average reader who enjoys reading when I get into a book. I love to read very funny or very sad books, also autobiographies.

I read three of your books *A Year Down Yonder, A Long Way from Chicago*, and *Fair Weather*. I loved all three of them because they took you into their world. I found out after reading how funny you are also how you foreshadow a very small part and then kind of give a clue on what happened. For example, my favorite clue was how Ellie Wilcox ended up being pregnant. And overall, the books were just down right funny.

When I was looking up information on you I came across a quote you had said. It went something like you never write a story without help from a child, so I want to help too. I think you should write a story about Mary Alice when she is grown up and how she acts and changes to be alike or different from her grandma and what her grandkids think of her. Or maybe the story should be about what the new grandkids think of the older grandma Dowdel when they come to visit.

After reading about you and your stories, I have some questions. When you were writing the stories *A Year Down Yonder* and *A Long Way from Chicago* was Joey posed to be you as a young boy? In *Fair Weather*, do you think that grandpa was you or a person that you wished to be. The reason that I am writing this letter . . .

Dana Zimmerman

ॐ ॐ ॐ

Dear Dana,

I'm glad to receive your letter and to know you have liked three of my books. Now I hope you find the new one, *The River Between Us*. It has some mystery in it and maybe more tears than laughter. I like it though.

Yes, I am Granddad in *Fair Weather*. Of course I'm all my characters, but especially him. If I had grandchildren, I would hope to embarrass them a lot.

But Joey wasn't especially me at his age. I wasn't quite his generation, and I never dreamed of being a pilot. I do have a younger sister, though, so that relationship was easy and natural to write. I'm glad you didn't ask if Grandma Dowdel is my grandma. When you're a writer, you can give yourself the grandma you *wish* you'd had.

I can't cook, and hope never to learn. This is my only recipe: Take a handful of characters and stir them into trouble over a hot fire. Then serve the survivor.

Sincerely,
Richard Peck

Todd Strasser

Dear Todd Strasser,

Hi, my name is Lauren from Mrs. Waltz's sixth-grade reading class. I love your *Help!* series, especially, *Help! I'm Trapped in My Sister's Body*. It was very funny when Jake had to kiss his sister's boyfriend since he was in his sister's body. I was laughing so hard that my stomach started to hurt! Another great book you wrote that I loved was *Help! I'm Trapped in Obedience School Again*. I was on the edge of my seat wondering how Josh was going to get out of this one when the police officer stopped Josh because he was walking Jake like a dog and Jake was on his hands and knees. I was wondering if you have a yellow Labrador retriever, just like the dog Lance in the book.

I read that when you were in school you were a poor writer, a terrible speller, and didn't get any encouragement until you were in college. That is interesting to me because you are just like one of my other favorite authors, Roald Dahl. I think that it's great that people can overcome their grades in school and do the opposite of what people thought you would be doing to make a living. I consider you to be the best author because you make me laugh while I read your books, and that makes it fun to read. You also use cliffhangers and build suspense that makes me want to read more. I would love to ask a favor of you. What I'm asking is much more personal and special than an autograph or a picture . . .

Lauren Shapiro

ა ა ა

Lauren,

You wrote one of the best letters I have ever received.

Here are the answers to some commonly asked questions:

My ideas for books come from conflicts. A conflict is like a problem the main character has to solve to be happy. The story tells what he or she goes through in order to solve the problem. In *Help! I'm Trapped* books it's usually Jake who wants to get out of whatever body he's trapped in. In *Heavenly Litebody* series it's usually some boy problem that will require Heavenly's special brand of magic to solve.

I sometimes get ideas from my friends, but I never put people I know in my books. Being an author is both fun and hard work. Writing a book takes a lot of time and effort and a lot of rewriting. But in the end I have something I'm proud of, and that feels good.

My favorite subjects were math and science (weird for a writer). My favorite sports are tennis and surfing. My favorite color is blue and the food I like best is definitely pizza.

My favorite recipe is to buy a frozen pizza, place it in the microwave, and serve it with a Coke.

Todd Strasser

❦ Glossary of Cooking ❧ Terms and Staples

Al dente: Pasta that is cooked firm to the bite but not overcooked.

Batter: An uncooked mixture of liquid, flour, and other ingredients that can vary in consistency and usually be poured.

Beat: To mix two or more ingredients rapidly, in a circular motion, until mixture is smooth.

Blend: To mix thoroughly two or more ingredients until mixture is smooth.

Bouillon: A clear soup that is similar to a stock but richer in flavor.

Brown: To fry, broil, or bake until food is brown in color.

Bundt pan: A rounded baking pan with a tube in the middle and fluted sides.

Caster sugar: Name of a very fine sugar in Britain; named because the small grains fit through a sugar "caster" or sprinkler; not as fine as confectioners' sugar. Grinding granulated sugar for a couple of minutes in a food processor achieves the same results.

Chill: To place in refrigerator until food is thoroughly cold.

Chop: To cut into small pieces.

Chutney: A spicy relish of fruits and spices generally served with curry dishes.

Cilantro or **coriander:** A parsley-like herb.

Combine: To mix two or more ingredients together.

Confectioners' sugar: Powdered sugar used in baking and in uncooked frostings.

Core: To remove the central seed part of certain fruits, such as apples or pears.

Corn flour: Cornstarch; used to thicken sauces, puddings, and so forth.

Cream: To make soft, smooth, and creamy by beating.

Deep fry: To cover food with hot oil and cook.

Dice: To cut food into small cubelike pieces.

Drizzle: To pour liquid over food in a thin stream.

Eggs separated: To separate egg yolks from egg whites.

Fine herbs: A combination of three or four herbs such as parsley, chervil, chives, and tarragon. This blend can be made from dried herbs or fresh herbs that have been chopped very fine.

Fold: To gently mix light ingredients with a heavier mixture by using a spatula.

Garnish: To decorate food with edible slices of fruit or herbs.

Grate: To separate food into small particles by rubbing it across the teeth of a grater.

Green onion (scallion): Young onion with underdeveloped bulb and green leaves that are long and thin.

Grease: To rub the inside of a baking pan with butter, margarine, or spray to prevent food from sticking.

Grease and flour: After greasing the pan, adding flour to lightly coat the surface of the pan.

Knead: To work dough into a smooth texture by pressing and folding with the heels of your hands.

Littleneck: A Pacific coast clam, usually steamed.

Liquidize: To change solid foods into a liquid substance by using a blender.

Mash: To squash food with a fork or potato masher.

Mince: To cut or chop into very little pieces.

Muscovado sugar: A very dark sugar with a strong molasses flavor.

Pancetta: An Italian bacon that is cured with salt, pepper, and other spices but is not smoked. Bacon is a suitable substitute.

Pesto: Refers to an uncooked sauce made of finely chopped herbs and nuts.

Pinch: A measure approximate 1/16 teaspoon.

Porcini mushrooms: A rich, meaty flavored mushroom used to add flavor to tomato or cream sauces.

Preheat: To set oven to correct temperature prior to baking.

Roll out: Rolling dough with rolling pin to required thickness per recipe.

Scald: To heat milk or cream just below the boiling point until a skin forms on the surface.

Scallion: *see* green onion.

Scones: A type of quick bread similar to biscuits.

Serrano pepper: Very hot, small, thin, and pointy chili, approximately 2 inches long and 1/2 inch wide.

Shallot: An herb with a garlic-onion flavor; small and milder than an onion, but resembles garlic cloves.

Sieve: A meshed utensil with holes that lets liquids and smaller pieces pass through.

Sift: To put dry ingredients through a sifter or sieve.

Simmer: To stew gently, below or just at the boiling point.

Slice: To cut into thin segments.

Stir: To mix ingredients until well blended.

Stir-fry: To cook food quickly, Chinese-style, in a skillet or wok.

Stock: The liquid in which meat, poultry, fish, or vegetables have been cooked.

Sultanas: Light-colored, sundried, seedless grapes resembling golden raisins.

Sweat: To cook vegetables and seasonings over low heat to release their moisture and flavor.

Torte: Cake or meringue-type of dessert, usually rich in eggs and nuts.

Toss: To mix ingredients lightly without mashing them.

Tube pan: A round high-sided pan with a hollow center tube.

Vanilla sugar: Granulated sugar that is flavored with vanilla by enclosing it with a vanilla bean in an airtight jar.

Water bath: A method for baking something with a gentle heat. To make a water bath, set the dish you are making inside another larger baking dish, half fill the larger dish with water, and bake.

Whisk: To stir rapidly, using a whisk, to blend ingredients.

Wilt: To apply heat so as to cause dehydration and a droopy appearance.

❦ Appendix of ❧ Measurements

Measuring Ingredients

Butter: $\frac{1}{4}$ pound of butter or margarine measures $\frac{1}{2}$ cup or 8 tablespoons and is usually one stick.

Chocolate: Comes divided into squares usually weighing 1 ounce each. Available in unsweetened, semisweet, and sweet.

Flour: Sift the specified amount of flour needed, fill the measuring cup heaping full, and level the cup with the straight edge of a knife.

Sugar: Most sugars can be measured in measuring cups. Spoon into cup and level off with the straight edge of a knife. If recipe calls for packed sugar, measure sugar by packing it down lightly with spoon and then level off with knife.

Measuring Liquid Ingredients

1 cup = 8 fluid ounces

2 cups = 16 fluid ounces

4 cups = 1 quart

4 quarts = 1 gallon

Measuring Dry Ingredients

3 teaspoons = 1 tablespoon = $\frac{1}{2}$ ounce

4 tablespoons = $\frac{1}{4}$ cup = 2 ounces

5 tablespoons + 1 teaspoon = $\frac{1}{3}$ cup

8 tablespoons = $\frac{1}{2}$ cup = 4 ounces

12 tablespoons = $\frac{3}{4}$ cups = 6 ounces

16 tablespoons = 1 cup = 8 ounces

32 tablespoons = 2 cups = 16 ounces = 1 pound

Dry to Cooked Equivalents

Spaghetti and Linguine

4 ounces dry = 2–3 cups cooked

8 ounces dry = 4–5 cups cooked

16 ounces dry = 8–9 cups cooked

Penne

4 ounces dry = 2½ cups cooked

8 ounces dry = 4½ cups cooked

Egg Noodles

4 ounces dry = 2–3 cups cooked

8 ounces dry = 4–5 cups cooked

Oven Equivalents

Fahrenheit	Centigrade	Gas Mark
275	140	1
300	150	2
325	160	3
350	180	4
375	190	5
400	200	6
425	220	7
450	230	8

✌ Index of Recipes ✌

✑ Index of Authors ✑ and Students

Authors

Students

❦ About the Author ❧

Josephine M. Waltz has been a teacher in New Jersey since 1974. She obtained a masters degree in education in 1979 and has a reading specialist certificate. She has taught many subjects in grades 5–8. In addition to recently teaching gifted children, she is currently piloting an enrichment course for 6th graders. For the past seven consecutive years her students have won awards for writing in the New Jersey Council of Teachers of English Writing Contest. Jo has been a presenter on language arts and reading strategies at educational meetings.

In 1958 she emigrated with her Sicilian family from Buenos Aires, Argentina, to the United States. Her own recollection of having few books as a child inspired her to help raise money for children in need of books.

Jo lives in Belle Mead, New Jersey, with her husband Charlie, three teenage children, and her Old English Sheep dog, Moli, who was a constant companion while writing this book. Jo, an avid gardener, enjoys being an amateur photographer and spending time with her family. This is her first publication.